Transforming Karachi into a Livable and Competitive Megacity

DIRECTIONS IN DEVELOPMENT
Infrastructure

Transforming Karachi into a Livable and Competitive Megacity

A City Diagnostic and Transformation Strategy

WORLD BANK GROUP

Contents

Boxes

Figures

Maps

Tables

Preface

This Karachi City Diagnostic (KCD) report, *Transforming Karachi into a Livable and Competitive Megacity*, was prepared at the request of the government of Sindh, Pakistan, which requested analysis by the World Bank Group for strategic advice in improving the livability and competitiveness of Karachi. Toward this objective, the World Bank conducted a set of rapid assessments from 2014 to 2016 as part of a broader technical assistance to develop a multisector approach for city transformation.

The KCD is a comprehensive attempt to collect, curate, and present detailed data on the economy, livability, and key urban infrastructure of the city and to provide an overview of the challenges and opportunities faced by the Karachi Metropolitan Region. The diagnostic also presents requirements to bridge the infrastructure gap and improve the metropolitan region's economic potential. The KCD recognizes citywide challenges and will provide the basis for discussion with the city and provincial governments on key pathways toward the transformation of the Karachi Metropolitan Region into a livable, inclusive, and competitive city.

The research conducted for this report focused primarily on desk review, publicly available data sets and studies, data provided by the provincial government, and World Bank data. Where data were scarce, the team leveraged alternative sources of data, such as spatial land-use and nighttime-light maps derived from satellite imagery. Additional field research was conducted for selected chapters to triangulate findings from the desk review through focus group discussions, key informant interviews, and in-depth case studies. The rapid analysis for each sector was conducted between October 2015 and June 2016 by sector specialists at the World Bank, with the support of international and national consultants as needed. Each of the sectoral research teams drew from these studies to present highlights of the predominant issues, knowledge gaps, lessons from recent program experience, and key takeaways to inform the strategic planning for the city of Karachi.

The validation of the results took place through a series of consultations between May and August 2016, which included senior officials of the provincial government, civil society representatives, women's groups, and business community representatives.

Acknowledgments

This report was prepared by a team led by Peter Ellis (Lead Urban Economist), Jaafar Sadok Friaa (Program Leader, Sustainable Development, Pakistan), and Jon Kher Kaw (Senior Urban Specialist). It consolidates the work conducted under the Karachi Transformation Strategy and the Karachi Infrastructure Gaps Assessment.

The report was prepared under the guidance of Patchamuthu Illangovan (Country Director, Pakistan) and Ming Zhang and Catalina Marulanda (Practice Managers, South Asia Urban Unit). Paul Kriss (Global Lead, Infrastructure and Services) provided peer review support for this report.

Core members of the team included Sohaib Athar (Urban Specialist) and Annie Bidgood (Urban Specialist).

Analyses and chapters were contributed by Masroor Ahmad (Senior Water and Sanitation Specialist), Moazzam Ahmed (Senior Country Officer, IFC), Sandra Cointreau (Consultant), Jana El-Horr (Social Development Specialist), Claire Kfouri (Senior Water and Sanitation Specialist), Haris Khan (Senior Disaster Risk Management Specialist), James Monday (Senior Environmental Engineer), Ghazala Mansuri (Lead Economist), Akiko Nakagawa (Senior Environmental Specialist), Jane Park (Consultant), Mark Roberts (Senior Urban Economist), Connor Spreng (Senior Economist), and Hasan Afzal Zaidi (Senior Transport Specialist).

Additional contributions were made to the preparation of the report by the following team members: Maha Ahmed (Rural Development Specialist), Sameer Akbar (Senior Environment Specialist), Farhan Anwar (Consultant), Shahnaz Arshad (Senior Urban Specialist), Shafick Hoossein (Environment Specialist), Muhammad Khalid (Consultant), Azheruddin Khan (Environmental Consultant), Sangmoo Kim (Urban Specialist), Hyunji Lee (Consultant), Fazal Noor (Consultant), Ahsan Imtiaz Paracha (Consultant), Uzma Quresh (Social Development Specialist), Jessica Schmidt (Urban Specialist), Wit Siemieniuk (Consultant), Deepali Tewari (Lead Urban Specialist), Fen Wei (Consultant), and Shahid Yusuf (Consultant). Michelle Lisa Chen and Ghulam Farid were the program assistants. Abdul Qadir provided assistance in organizing consultations with stakeholders.

The Korea Green Growth Trust Fund provided generous financial support for the preparation of this report.

Finally, the team would like to thank senior officials of the government of Sindh (GoS) and its various agencies and departments; the Karachi Metropolitan Corporation and other relevant agencies; members of the private sector, civil society, and academia; and other stakeholders that were consulted in preparing this report. The officials of the GoS Directorate of Urban Policy and Strategic Planning provided invaluable support in the preparation of this report.

Abbreviations

AGP	Auditor General of Pakistan
BRT	bus rapid transit
CDGK	City District Government Karachi
CPEC	China-Pakistan Economic Corridor
DBO	design-build-operate
DBOT	design-build-operate-transfer
DMA	District Management Authority
DHA	Defence Housing Authority
DMC	District Municipal Corporation
DRM	disaster risk management
EIA	environmental impact assessment
GDP	gross domestic product
GoS	government of Sindh
GVA	gross value added
JICA	Japan International Cooperation Agency
KCD	Karachi City Diagnostic
KDA	Karachi Development Authority
KE	Karachi Electric
KESC	K-Electric (formerly known as Karachi Electric Supply Company)
KMC	Karachi Metropolitan Corporation
KSDP	Karachi Strategic Development Plan
KWSB	Karachi Water and Sewerage Board
LG	local government
LQ	location quotient
MGD	million gallons per day
NRW	nonrevenue water
OECD	Organisation for Economic Co-operation and Development
OSR	own-source revenues
PPIAF	Public-Private Infrastructure Advisory Facility

PPP	public-private partnership
SBCA	Sindh Building Control Authority
SMTA	Sindh Mass Transit Authority
SSWMB	Sindh Solid Waste Management Board
UIPT	urban immovable property tax
WSS	water supply and sanitation

Executive Summary

Karachi is the largest city in Pakistan, with a population of 16 million.[1] It accounts for one-third of Sindh's population and one-fifth of the country's urban population. However, a highly complex political economy, highly centralized but fragmented governance, land contestation among many government entities, and weak institutional capacity have made it difficult to manage the city's development. Karachi has also been beset with a worsening security situation for the past few decades, although recent improvements in the security environment have led to a reduction in violent crime. Social exclusion of marginalized parts of the population is a challenge that requires immediate attention. These factors have resulted in the rapid decline of the city's quality of life and economic competitiveness from its thriving status after the country's independence.

Three Pathways for a City Diagnostic

The first part of this report provides a diagnosis of Karachi's issues, structured around three pathways focused on key aspects of city management (figure ES.1):

1. *City growth and prosperity*, in which the report analyzes the city's economy, competitiveness and business environment, and poverty trends
2. *City livability*, in which the report assesses the city's urban planning; city management, governance and institutional capacity, and municipal service delivery, focusing on three sectors—(i) public transport, (ii) water and sanitation, and (iii) municipal solid waste
3. *City sustainability and inclusiveness*, in which the report examines the city's long-term risks and resilience, looking at (i) fiscal management, (ii) environmental sustainability and the city's ability to deal with disasters and climate change, and (iii) social inclusion.

Each chapter provides a rapid diagnostic of the issues and a list of possible actions that can be taken in the short and long terms.

Figure ES.1 Framework of the Karachi City Diagnostic

Pathways for a city diagnostic	• City growth and prosperity • City livability • City sustainability and inclusiveness
Pillars for city transformation	• Building inclusive, coordinated, and accountable service-delivery institutions • Greening Karachi for sustainability and resilience • Leveraging Karachi's economic, social, and environmental assets • Creating a smart Karachi through policies and use of smart tools and technologies
Recommendations/tracks	• Create a shared vision for a livable, inclusive, and sustainable Karachi • Improve institutional governance and performance of city entities • Leverage public and private financing to meet Karachi's infrastructure needs

Karachi's Declining Economic Performance but Strong Poverty Reduction

Karachi is the country's financial and economic hub, generating 12–15 percent of Pakistan's gross domestic product (GDP), and is a powerhouse of manufacturing employment in the country. However, the city and its surrounding economic agglomeration are not generating economic productivity gains for the country. Evidence from nighttime lights—a strong proxy for economic activity—shows declining economic activity in the core areas of the city and high growth on its periphery, indicating that high-value economic activity is moving away from the city core (map ES.1). This stagnation of economic activity in the central areas is problematic for long-term economic and social potential. On the positive side, Karachi saw substantial poverty reduction in the 10 years up to 2015, with 9 percent of the city's population living in poverty in 2014–15 compared to 23 percent in 2004–05. This makes Karachi the least poor district in Sindh province and third least poor in Pakistan.[2] Despite this, there are pockets of high poverty and great variations in wealth within Karachi, due to its large physical and population size.

Karachi's Low Livability and Level of Basic Services

Karachi is ranked among the bottom 10 cities in the Global Livability Index. The city is very dense, with more than 20,000 persons per square kilometer. Urban planning, management, and service delivery have not kept pace with population growth, and the city seems to be headed toward a spatially unsustainable, inefficient, and unlivable form. Public open spaces and cultural heritage sites are under threat from commercial development. Urban green space is shrinking, and is now only 4 percent of the city's built-up area. All these are accompanied by insufficient basic services.

Map ES.1 Karachi's Pattern of Dimming Nighttime Lights at the Core, with Rapid Growth in Peripheral Areas, 1999 to 2010

Annual growth
- −0.238 – −0.092
- −0.092 – −0.038
- −0.038 – −0.006
- −0.006 – 0.016
- 0.016 – 0.032
- 0.032 – 0.043
- 0.043 – 0.064
- 0.064 – 0.097
- 0.097 – 0.145
- 0.145 – 0.237
- 0.237 – 0.378

0 5 10   20   30   40
km

Esri, HERE, DeLorme, Mapmyindia, © OpenStreetMap contributors, and the GIS user community

Source: World Bank analysis based on Defense Meteorological Satellite Program–Operational Line Scan System nighttime lights data.
Note: Data show annual average growth in nighttime light intensity from 1999 to 2010.

Public Transport

No cohesive transportation policy exists for Karachi, even as a thousand new vehicles are added to the roads each day. Traffic congestion and road safety are serious concerns. There is no official public transit system per se. An estimate says that 45 citizens compete for every bus seat, compared to 12 in Mumbai. Limited access to transit options affects women in particular. Karachi's transport problems cannot be resolved by simply investing in more infrastructure and facilities; the solution lies in a comprehensive strategy and efficient institutions.

Water, Sanitation, and Solid Waste

Karachi is experiencing a water and sanitation crisis that stems largely from poor governance. Financing for this sector is typically ad hoc and aimed at addressing immediate needs rather than long-term goals. Only 55 percent of water requirements are met daily. Rationing is widespread, and leakages and large-scale theft are common. Nonrevenue water can be as high as 60 percent, compared to 30 percent in Ho Chi Minh City and 17 percent in Manila. Many households rely on private vendors, who sell water from tankers at high prices. Less than 60 percent of the population has access to public sewerage, and almost all raw sewage is discharged untreated into the sea, along with hazardous and industrial effluent. Less than half of estimated solid waste is collected and transported to open dump sites, resulting in a major public health hazard.

Transforming Karachi into a Livable and Competitive Megacity
http://dx.doi.org/10.1596/978-1-4648-1211-8

Karachi's High Vulnerability to Disasters and Environmental Pollution

Karachi is at a high risk of natural and human-made disasters and is one of the most disaster-vulnerable districts in Pakistan. Various authorities responsible for disaster response suffer from weak coordination, information gaps, low capacity, and limited planning. Emergency response is hindered by poor land-use planning and building control. Regular flooding occurs during the annual monsoon season due to the poorly maintained and clogged drainage system. Air pollution is one of the most severe environmental problems. Environmental pollution has a high cost to public health, up to 7 percent of Sindh province's GDP.

Financing Requirements for Karachi's Infrastructure and Services Needs

This report estimates that Karachi needs around US$9 billion to US$10 billion in financing over a 10-year period to meet its infrastructure and service-delivery needs in urban transport, water supply and sanitation, and municipal solid waste. A full analysis of each sector is given in the body of the report.

However, current infrastructure spending by the public sector is well below these requirements, despite large recent increases. The availability of public financing for Karachi's needs is limited, which substantially increases its opportunity cost. Collections of the urban immovable property tax from Karachi (and Sindh) remain dismal compared to the potential. Global experience shows that the urban property tax is an important source of financing for cities. Punjab province collects four times as much in this tax as Sindh every year (figure ES.2). In comparison, a single metropolitan city in

Figure ES.2 Urban Property Tax Collection in Sindh Is Much Lower Than in Punjab (Pakistan) and Selected Indian Cities

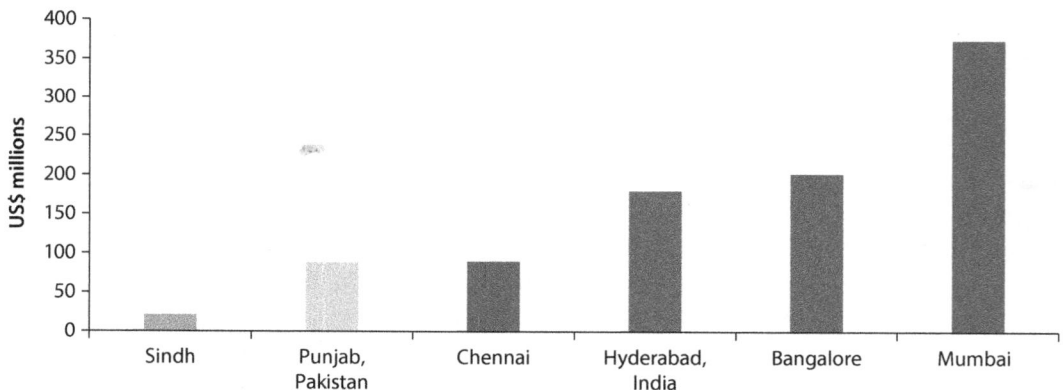

Source: World Bank analysis, based on official budget data for FY2015–16.

neighboring India collects many times more in annual property taxes than Sindh. Increasing revenue from this tax is essential to finance the infrastructure needs in Karachi.

Karachi's Inefficient and Weak City Governance Structure

Unclear roles, overlapping functions, and poor coordination among various agencies responsible for city governance and management have worsened the city's problems. Municipal and city development functions are highly fragmented, with roughly 20 agencies across federal, provincial, and local levels performing these functions, leading to a lack of coordinated planning and integration at the city level. These agencies also control nearly 90 percent of land in Karachi, but are reluctant to make it available for development. Public investment in infrastructure is reactive and uncoordinated, with a persistent focus on expansion of infrastructure over preventive maintenance or rehabilitation of existing assets. Elected local governments have weak systems and capacity and are not empowered to deliver many municipal functions. The provincial government retains substantial control over various city services and functions, such as master planning, building control, water and sewerage, solid waste management, and development of peri-urban and peripheral lands. Local governments are in an extremely weak financial position, relying almost solely on transfers from the provincial government to meet their budgetary needs, of which a majority is consumed by salaries and pensions, leaving precious little for much-needed maintenance or development of infrastructure.

The Way Forward: What Will It Take to Transform Karachi into a Livable and Competitive Megacity?

In addition to large-scale public and private financing, Karachi needs difficult reforms to improve its urban governance, institutional capacity, and coordination so that it can become a more economically productive and livable city. The second part of this report supplements four sector-specific issues and recommendations by providing the way forward based on four key pillars that will be important for the city's transformation:

1. *Building inclusive, coordinated, and accountable service-delivery institutions.* Create strong coordination mechanisms among various public land-owning and service-delivery agencies. Improve the ability of these agencies to plan, finance, and manage development programs. Empower local governments to take the lead in city management.
2. *Greening Karachi for sustainability and resilience.* Invest in environmentally sustainable infrastructure gaps and safeguard funds for its maintenance. Create mechanisms to protect vulnerable groups from the negative impacts of economic growth and climate change. Build a resilient and sustainable environment with an emphasis on livability and regeneration.

Transforming Karachi into a Livable and Competitive Megacity
http://dx.doi.org/10.1596/978-1-4648-1211-8

3. *Leveraging Karachi's economic, social, and environmental assets.* Involve the private sector in infrastructure provision by creating an enabling environment via policy reforms. Create incentives for more efficient performance by service-delivery agencies. Improve the ease of doing business and encourage public-private partnerships. Reduce delays and discretionary power for key business transactions under city and provincial authorities. Improve cost recovery and revenue collection for basic services while safeguarding vulnerable groups such as the poor. Leverage the city's land assets (such as state-owned land in prime locations) to finance critical infrastructure.

4. *Creating a smart Karachi through policies and the use of smart tools and technologies.* Innovate with smart policies to better manage city services, improve economic competitiveness, and facilitate engagement with citizens. Interventions should also focus on improving the ease of doing business to help enable economic growth and job creation.

The report underlines the structural nature of the city's problems and recommends a comprehensive, programmatic, and phased approach to strategically tackle these challenges. The four pillars of city transformation are accompanied by a set of actionable short- and long-term recommendations to transform Karachi. These recommendations can be categorized into three tracks (see figure ES.1):

Track 1: Create a shared vision for a livable, inclusive, and sustainable Karachi with a joint commitment across federal, provincial, and local governments that involves all key stakeholders, such as civil society, the private sector, and vulnerable groups, including women, the poor, and youth.

Track 2: Improve institutional governance and performance of city entities with strong coordination mechanisms among public land-owning and service-delivery agencies. Interventions should focus on reforms for accountability, strengthening contractual agreements between province-controlled municipal service agencies and local governments, and strengthening coordination among agencies across different levels of government.

Track 3: Leverage public and private financing to meet Karachi's infrastructure needs. Spending on infrastructure by the public sector in Karachi is well below required levels, despite large recent increases. The solution is to leverage significant and diverse sources of financing—both public and private.

In the short and medium terms, policy makers in Karachi need to focus on improving the use and efficiency of the following fiscal instruments to mobilize higher levels of financing:

1. Urban property tax
2. Enhanced conditional fiscal transfers to local governments
3. Management contracts with the private sector for municipal service delivery in the city

In the long term, policy makers must leverage more advanced sources of financing by creating an enabling environment via policy reforms and innovations, such as the following:

1. Explicit performance-based grants for local governments
2. Instruments for land-value capture, which will enable sharing in the benefits of increases in private land and property values due to infrastructure improvements, especially around planned mass transit stations
3. Subnational or municipal bonds, enhanced credit, and/or loan options through guarantees—such as those issued by sovereign entities or multilateral organizations—that will enable governments to obtain private and/or institutional financing
4. Innovative public-private partnerships, special-purpose vehicles, and infrastructure funds to invest in Karachi's needs

A full list of recommendations and proposed policy reforms for each sector and theme is available in the body of the report.

Notes

1. Population of Karachi Division (six districts), as per Population Census 2017 (Pakistan Bureau of Statistics, Government of Pakistan). Various unofficial sources estimate the city's population to be higher.
2. *District* here covers the entire Karachi administrative division, which includes six administrative districts. Data sources and methodology for all estimates are provided in the body of the report.

Transforming Karachi into a Livable and Competitive Megacity
http://dx.doi.org/10.1596/978-1-4648-1211-8

CHAPTER 1

City Context: Setting the Stage

Karachi's Recent Political, Social, and Physical Development

Karachi saw a rapid increase in population and economic activity in the decades after Pakistan's independence in 1947, and it became the political and economic hub of the country. The city spread outward rapidly to accommodate its new residents in planned formal and informal settlements and created a strong industrial base with the support of the state. However, multiple waves of migration since independence—due to various political, economic and security-related factors—have led to a diverse ethnic and social population mix in the city, which has led to conflict across multiple dimensions, at times with political and violent overtones. The city's security and livability have been further affected by the leading role it has played since the 1980s as a transit destination for people going to and from the conflict in Afghanistan and northwestern Pakistan, resulting in a proliferation of arms and drugs in a city (Hasan et al. 2015). Recent changes in the city's development include the following:

Population. The city's population has grown from just under 10 million in 1998 to 16 million in 2017, per official data.[1] The resulting changes in the demographic composition of the city have had major impacts on Karachi's politics, social fabric, and governance.

Poverty. World Bank staff estimates show that Karachi saw substantial poverty reduction from 2005 to 2015, with 9 percent of the city's population living in poverty in 2014–15 compared to 23 percent in 2004–05. This makes Karachi the least poor district in Sindh province and third least poor in Pakistan.[2] However, the low poverty rate masks the fact that Karachi is home to many people living in poverty, due to its size: 9 percent of Sindh's population living in poverty resides in Karachi. (This chapter provides more data and a methodological note on the poverty rate.)

Physical development. Most development is taking place on the periphery of the city, particularly in the Malir and West districts. Large formal housing schemes have gained momentum, while poor and vulnerable communities have become denser in the existing informal settlements and spread to new settlements on the periphery. There has been little coordination between the various land-owning agencies in the city on planning and development programs. As a result, the city's livability quality remains low, and Karachi is ranked as one of the least livable major cities in the world. The perennial shortage of housing in the city also continues to worsen, with at least 50 percent of the population living in informal settlements of varying quality (Hasan et al. 2015).

Economy. Karachi's economy centers on the manufacturing and trade sectors, rooted in the city's port, commercial centers in the historic core, and industrial areas developed since 1947. Karachi's economy has grown steadily in the past 18 years and per capita income has remained the highest in the country. Karachi's contribution to gross domestic product (GDP)—ranging from 11 to 20 percent, depending on the methodology used—and national tax revenue remains high. Growth in the real estate and construction sector has fluctuated in response to speculative activities, fueled in part by cash inflows from outside the city and the country. However, the competitiveness of Karachi's traditional sectors of manufacturing and trade is declining, especially relative to other cities.[3] The decline in the formal manufacturing sector has been accompanied by increased access to cheap imported goods, especially from China (Hasan and Raza 2015; Sayeed, Husain, and Raza 2016).

Institutions and devolution. From 2001 to 2010, the federal and provincial governments created the City District Government Karachi (CDGK) and devolved various powers of the provincial departments to the CDGK. However, this process has been effectively reversed since then, and the provincial government has taken over many functions of local governments, including Karachi, to run municipal activities. The previous elected mayor of the CDGK left office in 2010, and subsequent local government elections were held only after five years, in December 2015. Even then, the newly elected mayor did not assume office until August 2016. Institutional fragmentation and land contestations across government levels pervade Karachi. This has made it very difficult to manage the city's growth, in terms of both planning and project implementation. The inadequacy of institutional arrangements has also created gaps in governance and service delivery that have been filled by informal service providers and have exacerbated grievances among different social groups. If Karachi's growth is to be properly managed to boost growth and reduce poverty, greater coordination across the city's institutions, supported by an accountable and responsive local government, will be a key factor.

Social inclusion and security. The rapid growth of the Karachi metropolitan region has been accompanied by an increase in diversity and sometimes by the polarization of its social constituents, many of whom struggle to find adequate mechanisms of inclusion in the city's development process. Moving Karachi toward becoming a more livable city will require more inclusive governmental and administrative decision-making processes. While Karachi's security situation has worsened overall since the turn of the century, there have been some significant changes in operations by security agencies in the city since 2016, which have led to a reduction in violent crime and, to some degree, the containment of political and religious violence and criminal activity. Urban segregation and social exclusion, however, continue to be challenges that require immediate attention.

Service delivery. The aforementioned points have resulted in critical challenges to municipal service delivery, a proliferation of informal service providers, and deteriorating delivery in many sectors. The challenges include inadequate urban transport, water supply and sanitation, and solid waste management.

Rationale for a City Diagnostic

The Karachi City Diagnostic (KCD) is an initiative to collect, curate, and present detailed data covering the economy, infrastructure gaps, business environment, and social inclusion of the Karachi megacity. Its goal is to provide an integrated analysis of the challenges the city faces. This KCD is intended to assess the priorities and financing needs of the Karachi megacity, so it can make rapid progress in achieving the objectives of improving its economy, livability, and inclusiveness. The KCD concludes with a prioritization of the key challenges and identification of strategic directions for World Bank engagement and interventions.

If Karachi hopes to meet its economic and social development goals while improving the living conditions of its population, it is essential to prioritize and address the city's huge infrastructure gap, along with issues related to access, quality, and sustainability of the infrastructure. This is crucial for ensuring that governments make efficient, practical, and effective infrastructure development choices. All cities need high-quality infrastructure to facilitate the movement of people and goods and the delivery of basic services, and a better environment in which their populations can live, work, and innovate. But delivering these infrastructures and services in today's megacities is very challenging, and Karachi—like many megacities in South Asia—is no exception.

This KCD, therefore, focuses on the status of Karachi's key urban infrastructure, specifically, urban transport, water supply and sanitation, and municipal solid waste; the related deficits and proper targets for the future; bottlenecks to expansion and improvement; and recommendations for moving forward.

Conceptual Framework for the Karachi City Diagnostic

The Karachi City Diagnostic is focused on three main pathways:

Pathway 1: City growth and prosperity

Pathway 2: City livability

Pathway 3: City sustainability and inclusiveness

Notes

1. Population of Karachi Division (six districts), as per Pakistan Population Census 2017 by the Pakistan Bureau of Statistics. Various unofficial sources estimate the city's population to be higher.
2. The term *district* here covers the entire Karachi Division, which includes six administrative districts.
3. Based on an analysis of data from the Oxford Economics Competitive Cities database.

References

Hasan, Arif, Noman Ahmed, Mansoor Raza, Asiya Sadiq-Polack, Saeed Uddin Ahmed, and Moizza B. Sarwar. 2015. *Karachi: The Land Issue*. Oxford: Oxford University Press.

Hasan, Arif, and Mansoor Raza. 2015. "Impacts of Economic Crises and Reform on the Informal Textile Industry in Karachi." International Institute for Environment and Development working paper. London.

Sayeed, Asad, Khurram Husain, and Syed Salim Raza. 2016. *Informality in Karachi's Land, Manufacturing, and Transport Sectors: Implications for Stability*. Washington, DC: U.S. Institute of Peace Press.

CHAPTER 2

Pathway 1: City Growth and Prosperity

City Economy

Karachi's overall importance to Pakistan's economy is reflected in its superior gross domestic product (GDP) per capita and relatively high level of labor productivity. In 2012, Karachi generated at least 11.4 percent of national GDP and accounted for almost 5.5 percent of domestic employment, according to one estimate.[1] GDP per capita in the city was nearly 44 percent higher than the national level. The city's gross value added (GVA) per worker in 2012 was more than twice that of Pakistan overall.[2] Among major Pakistani cities, its level of GVA per worker was second only to that of Hyderabad. Karachi's relatively high level of labor productivity can be partly attributed to the overall size of its economy—in 2012, employment in Karachi exceeded that in Lahore, Pakistan's second-largest city, by 81 percent. Karachi's large size facilitates the exploitation of powerful agglomeration economies.

The city is a manufacturing-employment powerhouse. Its manufacturing base includes not just traditional labor-intensive industries but also heavier and more advanced businesses. In the formal economy, during 2005–6 Karachi accounted for about 42 percent of national employment in the motor vehicles and transport equipment sector; 35 percent in the metals, machines, and electronics sector; 32 percent in the chemical products sector; 21 percent in the wood products sector; 18 percent in the textiles sector; and 8 percent in the food and beverages sector.[3]

Geographically, Karachi forms an economically important corridor of manufacturing employment with the adjoining districts of Hyderabad, Thatta, and Lasbela (the last containing the industrial town of Hub adjacent to Karachi). These three districts and Karachi (which is technically a division) account for as much as 71 percent of national manufacturing employment in the formal sector in the motor vehicles and transport equipment sector; 41 percent in the metals, machines, and electronics sector; 39 percent in the chemical products sector; and 15 percent in the food and beverages sector.

However, Karachi's relatively high GDP growth, led by employment growth, has been accompanied by anemic productivity growth. While Karachi's real GDP grew 5.7 percent per annum from 2000 to 2012 (compared to 4.5 percent national growth), and employment likewise expanded at an impressive rate of 5.1 percent per annum, real per capita GDP grew at only 2.7 percent per annum. Labor productivity, as measured by GVA per worker, grew at an even more anemic rate of 0.47 percent per annum, which was less than half the rate of labor productivity growth nationally. Despite its manufacturing strengths, Karachi's competitiveness is declining compared to other cities in Pakistan.

This suggests that the city has been able to absorb increased labor only through the expansion of relatively low-productivity jobs. Slow productivity growth may also be associated with the city's struggle to adequately deal with the congestion associated with the rapidly increasing population and growing densities throughout much of the city, especially in its central commercial areas and other large job centers (map 2.1).

There is also evidence to suggest that Karachi's economic growth may have stalled. While the intensity of nighttime lights within 40 kilometers of the city's center grew rapidly between 2000 and 2004, it declined between 2004 and 2010. This is consistent with Karachi's speculative property and land boom between 2000 and 2007. This boom fueled the growth of the construction sector and stimulated demand for low-skilled labor. Between 2000 and 2010, Karachi experienced

Map 2.1 Population Densities Have Been Increasing around Karachi's Main Commercial and Job Centers, 1998 and 2010

a. 1998

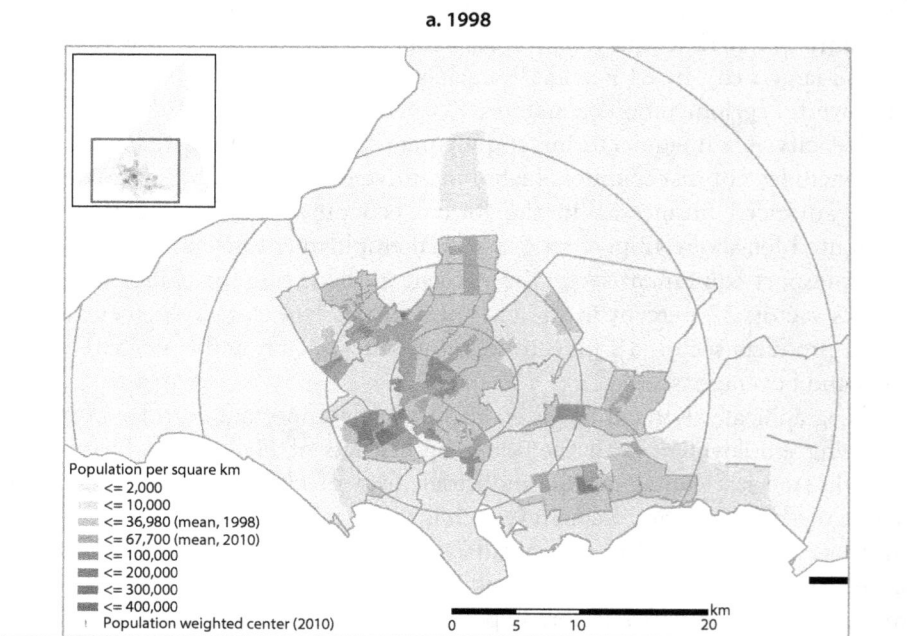

Population per square km
  <= 2,000
  <= 10,000
  <= 36,980 (mean, 1998)
  <= 67,700 (mean, 2010)
  <= 100,000
  <= 200,000
  <= 300,000
  <= 400,000
  Population weighted center (2010)

0   5   10   20 km

Map continues next page

Map 2.1 Population Densities Have Been Increasing around Karachi's Main Commercial and Job Centers, 1998 and 2010 *(continued)*

b. 2010

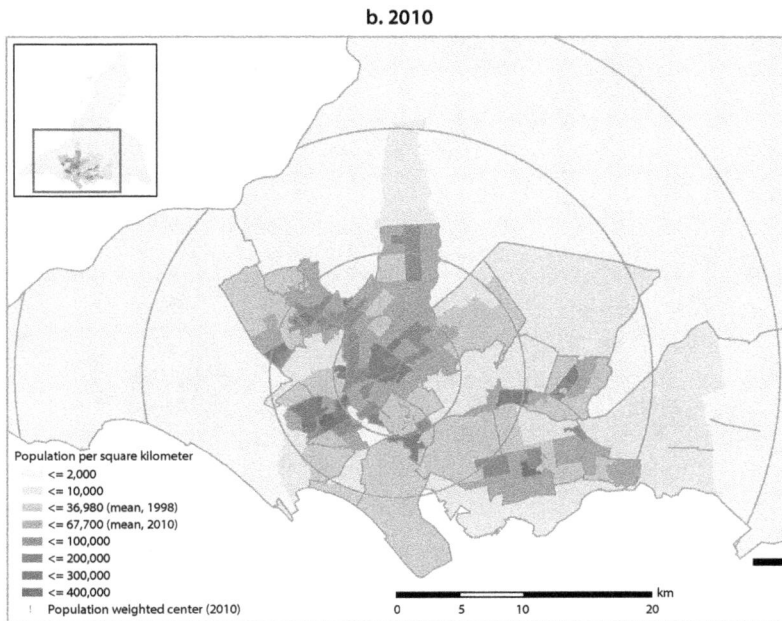

Population per square kilometer
- <= 2,000
- <= 10,000
- <= 36,980 (mean, 1998)
- <= 67,700 (mean, 2010)
- <= 100,000
- <= 200,000
- <= 300,000
- <= 400,000
- Population weighted center (2010)

km
0   5   10   20

Sources: World Bank analysis based on 1998 Population Census and JICA 2010–11 Karachi Household Survey. Data at Union-Council level.

an absolute decline in nighttime light intensities within 11 kilometers of its center, which was offset by growth at distances greater than 11 kilometers (map 2.2).[4] This stagnation of economic activity in the central areas of the Karachi is worrisome for the city's long-term economic and social potential; it indicates that high-value economic activity is moving away from the city's core. Policies to revitalize and rejuvenate city cores are of critical importance.

Overview of the Current Structure of the City's Economy

The manufacturing and trade sectors dominate employment in Karachi. They account for 63 percent of overall employment in the city (figure 2.1). Public administration, transport and telecommunications, and health and education also account for notable shares of local employment.

Although small in terms of employment share, the finance and real estate sector is estimated to have generated 13.2 percent of Karachi's overall GVA in 2012.[5] The sector has made an important contribution to Karachi's GDP growth over the past decade and a half, especially the decade up to 2010, when formal sector credit to the private sector increased substantially, including commercial lending (Government of Pakistan 2015). It is unclear, however, to what extent the contribution of the real estate sector has been based on unsustainable speculation in property and land markets, as opposed to economic fundamentals.

Map 2.2 Karachi's Slow Nighttime Light Growth or Dimming at the Core and Rapid Growth in Peripheral Areas, 1999–2010

Annual growth
- −0.238 – −0.092
- −0.092 – −0.038
- −0.038 – −0.006
- −0.006 – 0.016
- 0.016 – 0.032
- 0.032 – 0.043
- 0.043 – 0.064
- 0.064 – 0.097
- 0.097 – 0.145
- 0.145 – 0.237
- 0.237 – 0.378

0 5 10   20   30   40
km

Esri, HERE, DeLorme, MapmyIndia, © OpenStreetMap contributors, and the GIS user community

Source: World Bank analysis based on Defense Meteorological Satellite Program–Operational Line Scan System nighttime lights data.
Note: The data show annual average growth in nighttime light.

Figure 2.1 Manufacturing and Trade Sectors Dominate Karachi's Economy

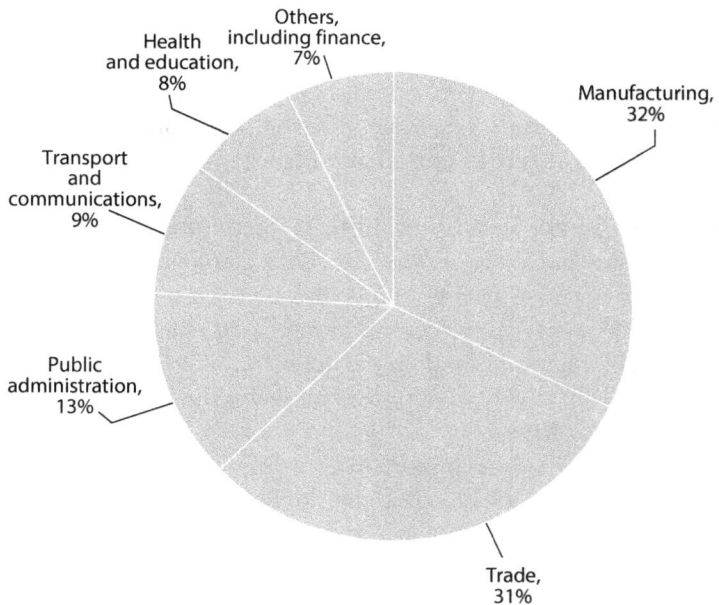

- Others, including finance, 7%
- Health and education, 8%
- Transport and communications, 9%
- Manufacturing, 32%
- Public administration, 13%
- Trade, 31%

Source: World Bank analysis, based on JICA 2010–11 Karachi Household Survey.

Karachi's Evolving Patterns of Specialization

The finance and real estate sectors are important for Karachi's future development. This is reflected in the particularly high location quotient[6] (LQ) of 7.3 in the finance and real estate sector (map 2.3). Karachi also exhibits high LQs in the manufacturing, public administration, trade, transport and communications, health, and education sectors. For each of these, the share of local employment is more than twice the share of national employment.

However, it appears that Karachi has been losing competitiveness in all its traditional sectors of specialization. With the exception of the dynamic but small finance and real estate sector, Sindh province experienced declining LQs across all its key nonagricultural sectors between 1999 and 2011. A particular cause of concern is the decline in the LQ for the manufacturing sector (figure 2.2). Informality in employment is also increasing across most sectors, including manufacturing. The decline in the formal manufacturing sector has also been accompanied by increased access to cheap imported goods, especially from China (Hasan and Raza 2015; Sayeed, Husain, and Raza 2016).

Map 2.3 Sector Locations on Karachi

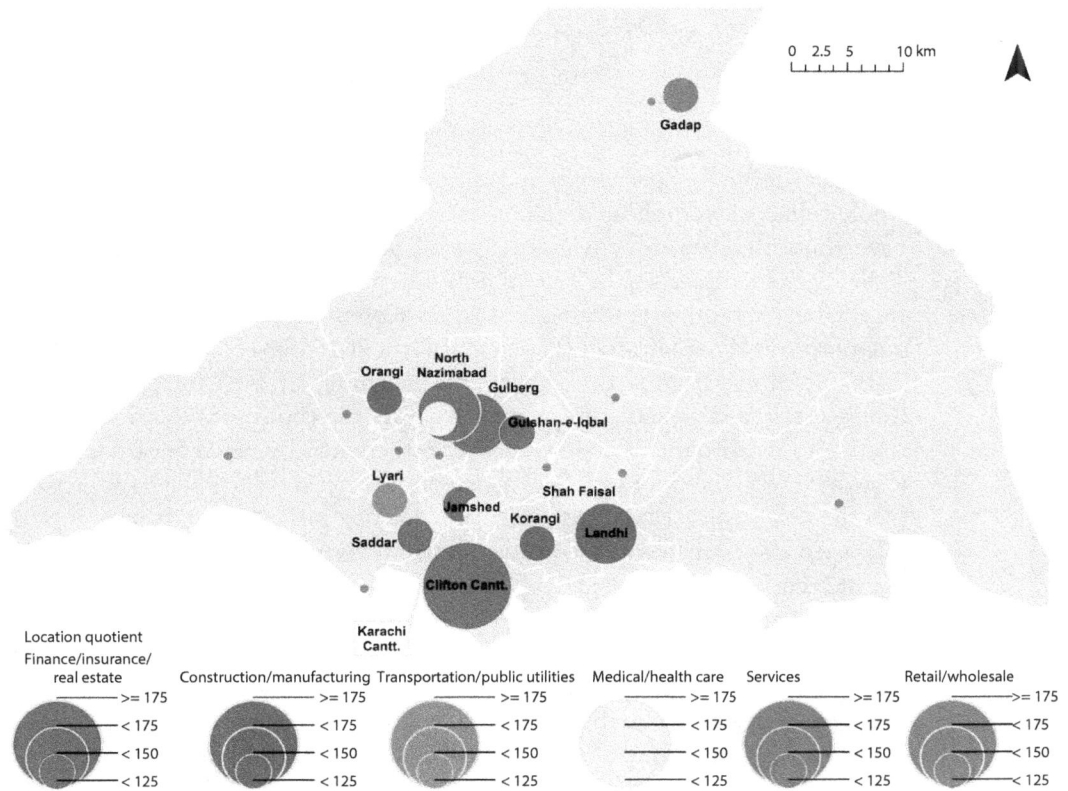

Source: Labor Force Survey data (2008–11 editions), reported in World Bank 2014.

Figure 2.2 Finance and Real Estate Sectors Emerge as Key Growth Drivers as Manufacturing Stalls

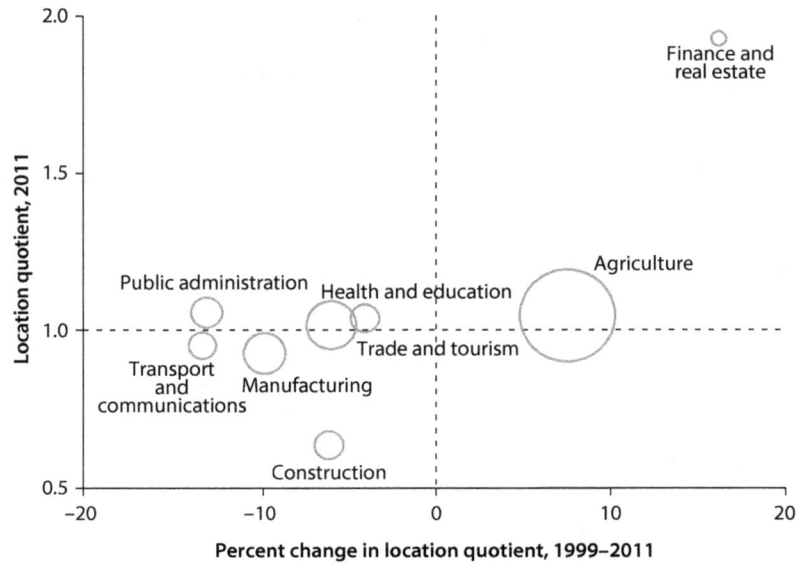

Source: Analysis of Labor Force Survey data, as reported in World Bank 2014.

Key Constraints

Karachi's declining specialization in manufacturing relative to Pakistan as a whole reflects a complicated combination of internal and external factors that have contributed to the city's slow overall pace of labor productivity growth. The city has suffered in the face of stiff international competition, particularly from China and other emerging East Asian economies, in its traditional areas of manufacturing specialization (Hasan and Raza 2015; Sayeed, Husain, and Raza 2016). It suffers from several constraints, including (i) frequent power supply shortages; (ii) a large and growing infrastructure gap (both in absolute terms and relative to industrial clusters in Punjab), exacerbated by heightened congestion associated with the city's rapidly growing population and declining basic services; (iii) the city's political situation; and (iv) violence and criminal activity, specifically extortion, targeted at the private sector.[7] This may have improved with the recent security operation.

The criminal activity has its origins partially in the informality that pervades Karachi's land market, exacerbated by the boom in property and land prices. Karachi's industrial estates have also become increasingly less "sensible" locations for industrial activity, as Karachi's population, driven to a significant extent by internal immigration, has swelled and the built-up area has expanded outward (Hasan et al. 2015; Sayeed, Husain, and Raza 2016). In this sense, Karachi is also being constrained by historical decisions about the location of the industrial estates.

Because of the country's declining international competitiveness, the dynamics of manufacturing locations within Pakistan have come to be increasingly determined by the domestic market. Karachi has suffered a loss of manufacturing activity to Punjab province, where the domestic business cluster largely exists. Informality is also a constraint on Karachi's overall economic performance. Although formal sector employment accounts for a larger share of the workforce in Karachi than in other Pakistani cities, the informal sector nevertheless accounted for 67 percent of overall employment in the city in 2011, according to one estimate.[8]

Other constraints on Karachi's overall economic performance include the low level of the female labor force participation. Only 8.5 percent of working-age females in Sindh's cities are part of the labor force—with Karachi having the highest number among cities in the province by far. This is low compared to 14 percent in Punjab and identical to Khyber Pakhtunkhwa (KP) province (8.5 percent). Among men, Sindh cities have a rate of labor force participation comparable to other provinces.[9] Analysis of recent household survey data conducted by the Japan International Cooperation Agency shows a striking gender imbalance in the distribution of the employed population in Karachi (figure 2.3), a trend that is not unique to the city but is worrisome given its substantial economic and employment potential. Policy measures must reduce specific constraints on women's participation in the labor market in Karachi. These constraints include, but are not limited to, inadequate, unreliable, and

Figure 2.3 Ratio of Employed Persons to Working-Age Population by Age and Gender Shows that Female Employment Is Extremely Low in Karachi

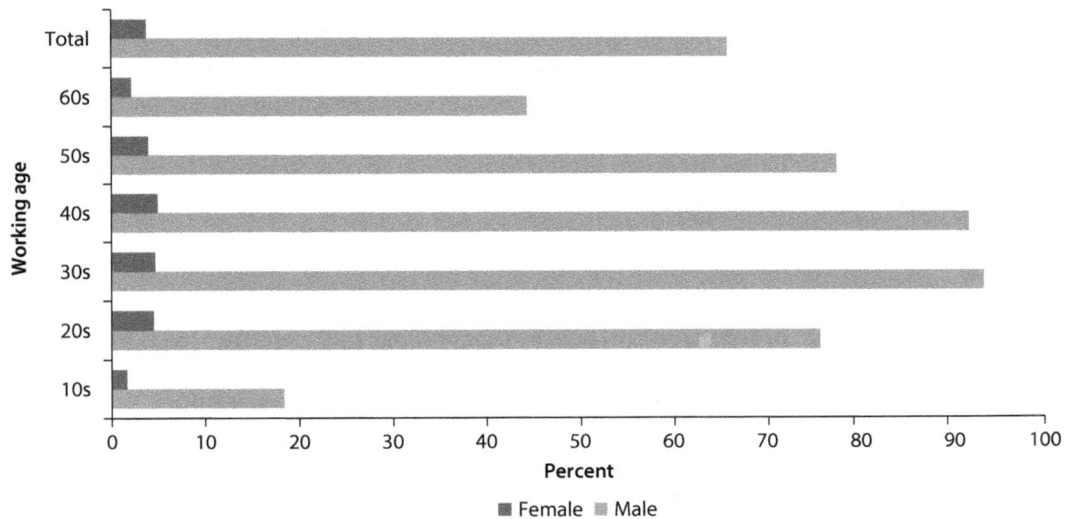

Source: World Bank analysis based on JICA 2010–11 Karachi Household Survey.
Note: Total working-age population in sample is 148,084, out of which the total of employed persons is 54,591. This excludes the following categories from the working-age population: students (28,754); unemployed or retired (9,755); those reporting job type or profession as housewives (54,594); and workers in primary sector (390).

Transforming Karachi into a Livable and Competitive Megacity
http://dx.doi.org/10.1596/978-1-4648-1211-8

unsafe public transport for women that reduces their opportunities to access jobs, education, and civic opportunities; unsafe public spaces, with a likelihood of harassment and violence; and an absence of gender-responsive infrastructure, such as affordable day care centers and working women's hostels. These constraints limit women's access to jobs, education, and civic opportunities.

The links between the city of Karachi and Sindh province are critical for job creation and economic growth. Building an enabling environment requires careful analysis of how the city's economy is linked to and interacts with the provincial economy—other urban centers and rural Sindh. Many of the key reforms for improving private sector competitiveness will have to be initiated and implemented at the provincial level, and this necessitates an assessment of how such reforms will impact the provincial economy beyond Karachi.

Business Environment

Karachi needs economic growth to sustain itself, restore the vitality of its local economy, absorb a growing labor force, and provide for its growing population. The city's private sector employs a significant proportion of the country's labor force, but private sector investment to GDP almost halved in 2015. The public sector has not yet been able to leverage and incentivize the private sector.

A poor investment climate constrains Karachi's growth. Businesses must deal with hindering policies and regulations (DfID, n.d.; World Bank and IFC 2015). Constraints include (i) a poor law-and-order environment; (ii) political instability; (iii) corruption; (iv) bureaucratic red tape; and (v) institutional deficiencies. In these challenges the private sector is hindered primarily where it is required to interact with the government.

The World Bank Enterprise Survey identifies corruption, political instability, and electricity shortage as the biggest obstacles to the business environment in Karachi.[10] The survey gathers and presents the perceptions of the private sector on the biggest obstacles to the business environment (see appendix A for key findings). Three areas stand out when Karachi is compared internationally, locally, and over time:

Corruption: 35 percent of the respondent firms identified corruption as the biggest obstacle to the business environment in 2013, in contrast to the global average of 6 percent and South Asian average of 9 percent. This is just as pronounced when Karachi is compared nationally with other provinces. The perception of corruption and its impact has deteriorated over time.

Political instability: 22 percent of the respondents identified political instability as the biggest obstacle, compared to 11 percent internationally. This perception has increased dramatically, from 2 percent in 2007, and points to a growing perception among Karachi's business owners and managers that the city is succumbing to policy uncertainty as politics is increasingly being carried out along ethnic, religious, and sectarian lines.

Electricity shortage: The survey points to electricity shortages as a significant obstacle, but this number has improved considerably over the years, from 64 percent of respondents identifying this as the biggest obstacle in 2007 to 14 percent in 2013.

The World Bank's *Doing Business* data indicate that the regulation of private sector firms in Karachi is relatively poor when compared nationally and internationally.[11] The data for Pakistan also provide important insights into the performance of Karachi agencies and officials when dealing with private firms (see appendix B for findings). Key findings are as follows:

Starting a business is time consuming. It takes 19 days (and 10 steps) to start a business in Karachi, higher than the South Asian average of 15.7 days (7.9 steps) and Organisation for Economic Development Co-operation (OECD) average of 8.3 (4.7 steps). The ease of starting a business across the dimensions of time, cost, steps, and paid-up minimum capital has been shown to be associated with investment and economic growth. A 10-day reduction in the time required to start a business is associated with a 0.3 percentage point increase in the investment rate and a 0.36 percent increase in the GDP growth rate in relatively poor but well-governed economies.[12]

Karachi has performed well on trade competitiveness compared to other Pakistani cities due to its port, but it pales internationally.[13] The typical container dwell time at Karachi's ports is a lengthy seven days, which is three times that of developed countries and East Asia, and there are significantly higher call charges: US$27,000, almost 10 times the amount in Singapore and Dubai. Inefficient trade facilitation and logistics have become steep barriers to regional competitors. Border and documentary compliance to export and import from Karachi took much longer than in and among OECD countries (appendix B).

The high cost of and limited access to land are constraining business activities and growth. Numerous federal and provincial government agencies own, control, or manage Karachi's land (see appendix E). Only 1.5 percent of all land in Karachi is being used for commercial activities. Growth in commercial activity is hindered because of unclear property rights and a lack of transparency, in part due to the absence of a central land registration authority. Thus, Karachi ranks low on construction permits and property registration (appendix B).

Paying taxes is time consuming. Over the past decade, the frequency of tax payments for limited liability companies in Karachi has remained at 47 payments per year (consuming 594 hours), significantly higher than the South Asian average of 31 (299 hours) and the OECD average of 11 (177 hours).

Overall, Karachi's performance fares poorly in the areas that deal with private firms' contact with the government. Karachi has yet to catch up with cities internationally, as well as other cities in Pakistan. Across the dimensions of corruption, political instability, crime (and contact or not with law enforcement), regulations, and tax administration.

Private-sector-led growth will benefit from interventions and reforms beyond the regulatory environment. While the regulation of the private sector and inter-actions of private firms with the government are in urgent need of reform, greater investment and competitiveness in the private sector can be encouraged. From support for individual sectors or subsectors, to improving linkages between firms in Karachi and firms in all of Sindh province or beyond, the use of multiple instruments should be considered for catalyzing needed improvements in eco-nomic performance.

Poverty

World Bank staff estimates indicate that Karachi saw substantial poverty reduction from 2005 to 2015, with 9 percent of the city's population living in poverty in 2014–15 compared to 23 percent in 2004–05. This makes Karachi the least poor district in Sindh province and third least poor in Pakistan[14] (figure 2.4).

However, the low poverty rate masks the fact that Karachi is home to many people living in poverty, due to its size: 9 percent of Sindh's popula-tion living in poverty resides in Karachi. Further, since the Karachi Division is further divided into six districts, there can be significant differences in living standards and access to basic services across the city, and aggregate city-level statistics tend to conceal these patterns. There are pockets of high poverty in Karachi. Given the city's size, household data at a more granular level are needed to understand the persistence and dynamics of poverty within Karachi over time. See box 2.1 for more information on determining poverty in the city.

Figure 2.4 Trend in Poverty Headcount in Karachi Districts

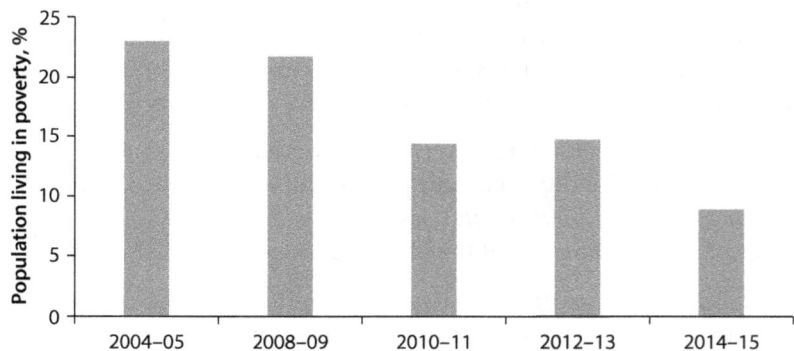

Source: World Bank estimation.

Box 2.1 Methodological Note on District-Level Estimation of the Poverty Rate

The poverty headcount in Pakistan is estimated using the Household Income and Expenditure Survey (HIES), which is statistically representative at the national, provincial, and rural-versus-urban levels. As the HIES does not go below the provincial level in terms of statistical representation, estimates of poverty at a more disaggregated level, such as a district or a city, cannot be obtained from the HIES directly. The most effective approach is to use the best available instrument that collects data that are statistically representative at the district level, has enough variables that are common to the HIES, and is conducted in the field around the same time as the HIES. In Pakistan, the Pakistan Social and Living Standards Measurement (PSLM) survey satisfies these conditions and can therefore be used to estimate poverty at the district level using small-area estimation techniques. Five HIES-PSLM pairs have been used to estimate trends in district poverty levels. The pairs used include data for the following years: 2006–07 (HIES 2005–06 and PSLM 2006–07); 2008–09 (HIES 2007–08 and PSLM 2008–09); 2010–11 (HIES 2010–11 and PSLM 2010–11); 2012–13 (HIES 2011–12 and PSLM 2012–13); and 2014–15 (HIES 2013–14 and PSLM 2014–15).

Notes

1. Analysis of data from the Oxford Economics (2014), *Global Cities Database*. Another estimate by the World Bank (2014) of Karachi's contribution to national GDP is 14.5 percent in 2010.

2. GVA measures the difference between output and intermediate consumption. It therefore measures the value of goods and services that have been produced, less the cost of all inputs and raw materials that are directly attributable to that production.

3. Based on Census of Manufacturing Industries 2005–06, Pakistan Bureau of Statistics, Government of Pakistan (2006).

4. Changes in nighttime light intensity over time are considered a strong proxy for economic growth and can be used in the absence of subnational data.

5. Based on data from Oxford Economics (2014), *Global Cities Database*.

6. Insights into the structure of Karachi's economy can be provided through LQ analysis. The LQ measures an industry's share of local employment relative to its share of national employment. Where the LQ for a given industry exceeds one, this indicates that the local economy is more specialized in that industry than the national economy overall. Conversely, an LQ of less than one indicates that the local economy is less specialized in an industry than the national economy overall. Findings are based on Labor Force Survey data for various years, as reported in World Bank (2014).

7. According to interviews of researchers conducted by the World Bank in December 2015, this criminal activity has constrained the growth of individual manufacturing enterprises and encouraged informality, as business owners seek to avoid becoming visible targets for extortion.

8. Analysis of Labor Force Survey data, as reported in World Bank 2014.

9. Augmented labor force for age 10 and above. The trends are similar for the nonaugmented labor force, but with lower rates of female participation: Sindh, 6.2 percent; Punjab, 12.8 percent; and KP, 8.3 percent—according to the *Labor Force Survey* of 2014–15. Determining the underlying drivers behind low female labor force participation in Karachi are beyond the scope of this report and warrant further analysis.

10. The term "political instability" is used here as per the methodology of the World Bank Enterprise Surveys conducted around the world. The results presented are for the entire province of Sindh. However, given that approximately 89 percent of the respondents surveyed in Sindh were based in Karachi, it can be extrapolated that the results for Sindh are also valid for Karachi.

11. Doing Business captures the key constraints to private sector investment based on an analysis of quantitative data.

12. Based on World Bank Doing Business indicators, including subnational data on Pakistan, as reported in World Bank (2009, 2011).

13. Based on the Trading Across Borders indicator.

14. The term *district* here covers the entire Karachi Division, which includes six administrative districts.

References

DfID (Department for International Development). N.d. "Investment Climate Core Brief." London: DfID.

Government of Pakistan. 2015. *Pakistan Economic Survey, 2014–15.* Islamabad.

Hasan, Arif, Noman Ahmed, Mansoor Raza, Asiya Sadiq-Polack, Saeed Uddin Ahmed, and Moizza B. Sarwar. 2015. *Karachi: The Land Issue.* Oxford: Oxford University Press.

Hasan, Arif, and Mansoor Raza. 2015. "Impacts of Economic Crises and Reform on the Informal Textile Industry in Karachi." International Institute for Environment and Development Working Paper. London.

JICA (Japan International Cooperation Agency). 2011. *Karachi Household Survey 2010–2011.* (Note that the survey did not appear in a formal publication.)

Oxford Economics. 2014. *Global Cities Database.* Wayne, PA.

Pakistan Bureau of Statistics, Government of Pakistan. 2006. *Census of Manufacturing Industries, 2005–06.* Islamabad.

———. Various years. *Labor Force Survey.* Islamabad.

Sayeed, Asad, Khurram Husain, and Syed Salim Raza. 2016. *Informality in Karachi's Land, Manufacturing, and Transport Sectors: Implications for Stability.* Washington, DC: U.S. Institute of Peace Press.

World Bank. 2009. *Doing Business 2010: Reforming through Difficult Times.* Washington, DC: World Bank, http://www.doingbusiness.org/reports/global-reports /doing-business-2010.

———. 2011. *Doing Business 2012: Doing Business in a More Transparent World.* Washington, DC: World Bank, http://www.doingbusiness.org/reports/global-reports /doing-business-2012.

———. 2014. "Pakistan Urban Sector Assessment." Background paper for South Asia Urbanization Flagship, unpublished report. Washington, DC: World Bank.

World Bank and IFC (International Finance Corporation). 2015. *Enterprise Surveys: Pakistan Country Profile 2013*. Washington, DC: World Bank and IFC.

CHAPTER 3

Pathway 2: City Livability

Karachi ranks low in livability. In 2015, it was in the bottom 10 cities (134 out of 140) in the Global Livability Index produced by the Economist Intelligence Unit. Benchmarking with comparator cities suggests that Karachi could do much better in terms livability and in the dimensions of health, environment, safety, and education (figure 3.1).

The following sections focus on the city's current state and examine critical gaps in (i) urban planning and policy; (ii) city management, governance, and institutional capacity; and (iii) municipal service delivery and living standards, highlighting urban transport, water supply and sanitation (WSS), and solid waste management. Preliminary recommendations for improvement can be found at the end.

Urban Planning and Policy

Urban Expansion and City Structure

Karachi's urban planning, management, and service delivery have been unable to keep pace with the needs of a rapidly growing population or in terms of quality of living and business environment. The Karachi metropolitan region covers an area of 3,600 square kilometers (km²), with a built-up area of approximately 1,600 km². It has grown from a city of 450,000 in 1941 to 16 million today (per official statistics).[1] The average population density in the existing urbanized area is 23,800 persons per km², which is relatively high compared to other big cities in the world (figure 3.2). It is estimated that the urban area will expand from 796 km² in 2013 to 1,580 km² in 2030.

The evolution of land-use patterns over the past 15 years suggests that Karachi is now at a tipping point and could be heading toward a spatially unsustainable, inefficient, and unlivable city form. Preliminary analysis of high-resolution satellite imagery using land-use mapping techniques reveals the following between 2001 and 2013 (see appendix C for a detailed map):

1. Karachi's urban footprint has grown 29 percent, an increase of about 145 km² in land area. Significant parts of Karachi appear to consist of land that is being

Figure 3.1 Karachi Lags Comparatively in Livability

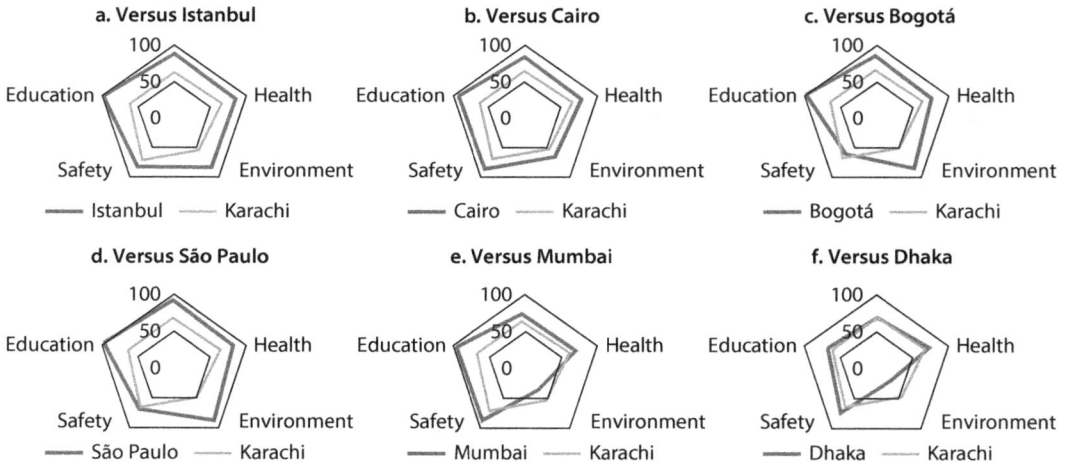

a. Versus Istanbul
b. Versus Cairo
c. Versus Bogotá
d. Versus São Paulo
e. Versus Mumbai
f. Versus Dhaka

Source: Livability index calculated by World Bank staff, based on Amirtahmasebi and Kim 2014.

Figure 3.2 Karachi Is Emerging as a Densely Populated City with a Low Quality of Life

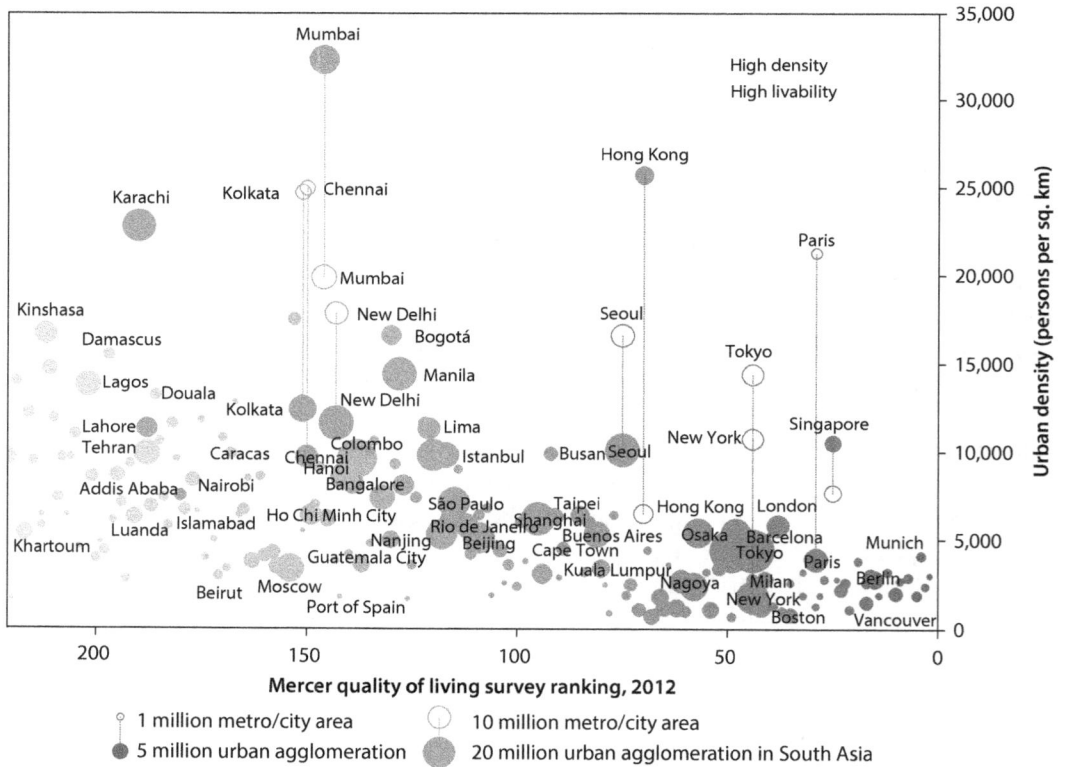

Mercer quality of living survey ranking, 2012

○ 1 million metro/city area   ◯ 10 million metro/city area
● 5 million urban agglomeration   ⬤ 20 million urban agglomeration in South Asia

Sources: World Bank analysis, based on ranking surveys by Mercer 2012; population density data from United Nations Statistical Division 2014 and Demographia World Urban Areas 2014.
Note: A lower ranking means higher livability.

prepared for development (20 percent in 2001, 22 percent in 2013), both on the periphery and within the city core (map 3.1).[2] Only about 40 percent of the 118 km^2 of land under construction in 2001 was converted to other urban land uses by 2013. This could suggest constraints on construction and implementation.

2. Large prime locations in the city core remain underdeveloped and underleveraged despite the rapid expansion on the periphery. Currently, prime waterfront area has not been developed (about 12 km^2 of land in 2013), even though the road network has been in place for over 10 years.[3] It is not clear how the city plans to fully leverage the potential of prime waterfront land, other than for exclusive, high-end residential enclaves.

3. Rapid development is observed on the north and northeast periphery of the city, and large developments have started to "leapfrog" beyond the city core. In 2013, developments belonging to housing societies, and satellite towns such as Bahria Town, started to develop beyond the city.

4. New development of land is being carried out independently by various land-owning agencies at different government levels. For example, the Clifton/ Defense Housing Authority (DHA) (city core) is under federal-military control, Malir (northeast) is under provincial control, and cooperative housing societies are regulated by the city government.

5. Urban green areas have declined as a proportion of the urban footprint, from 4.6 percent (27 km^2) to 3.7 percent (30 km^2).[4] It is significant that even though the green land areas have increased slightly, their proportion of the urban footprint has decreased.

Map 3.1 Many Areas in Karachi Exhibit Land Being Prepared for Development by Various Agencies

a. 2001   b. 2013

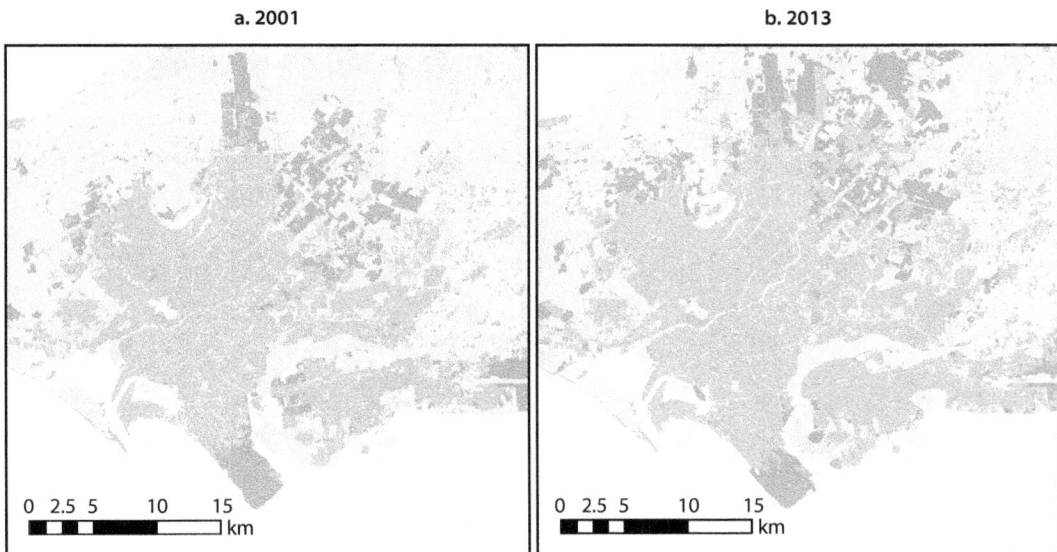

Source: World Bank analysis, based on satellite imagery and land-use classification from the European Space Agency.
Note: Pink shade shows area under development.

Transforming Karachi into a Livable and Competitive Megacity
http://dx.doi.org/10.1596/978-1-4648-1211-8

Based on an analysis of the Japan International Cooperation Agency's (JICA's) Karachi Household Survey 2010–11, jobs are highly concentrated within the city center, where the high-income population lives. These centrally located opportunities are high-skill-level jobs, while low-skill jobs tend to be more dispersed (map 3.2). As the city expands to accommodate a growing population, travel from housing locations on the periphery becomes costly and time consuming, which has a significant impact on the poor who live on the periphery (map 3.3). There may be a need to revisit the Karachi Strategic Development Plan (KSDP) 2020's spatial development strategy of bringing jobs and a mix of uses closer to the population and housing schemes on the periphery.

City and Regional Planning

It is estimated that over 50 percent of Karachiites live in informal settlements, which grow at twice Karachi's annual urban growth rate (Hasan et al. 2015). Other estimates show that the current demand of 80,000 housing units is met by a supply of only 30,000 units per year in the formal sector. The gap is made up for with the supply of at least 32,000 housing units in *katchi abadis* (informal settlements) annually (Hasan 2013). This is coupled with decades of inadequate

Map 3.2 Distribution of Jobs, Skilled Labor, and Unskilled or Semiskilled Labor across Karachi Shows a Spatial Mismatch between the Location of Jobs and Where People Live as the City Expands

a. Jobs

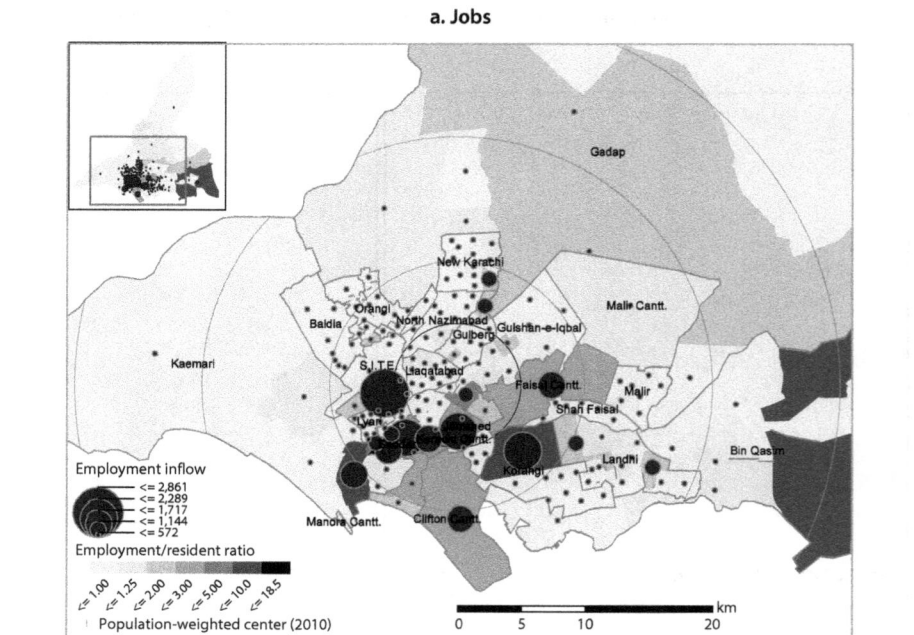

map continues next page

Map 3.2 Distribution of Jobs, Skilled Labor, and Unskilled or Semiskilled Labor across Karachi Shows a Spatial Mismatch between the Location of Jobs and Where People Live as the City Expands *(continued)*

b. Skilled labor

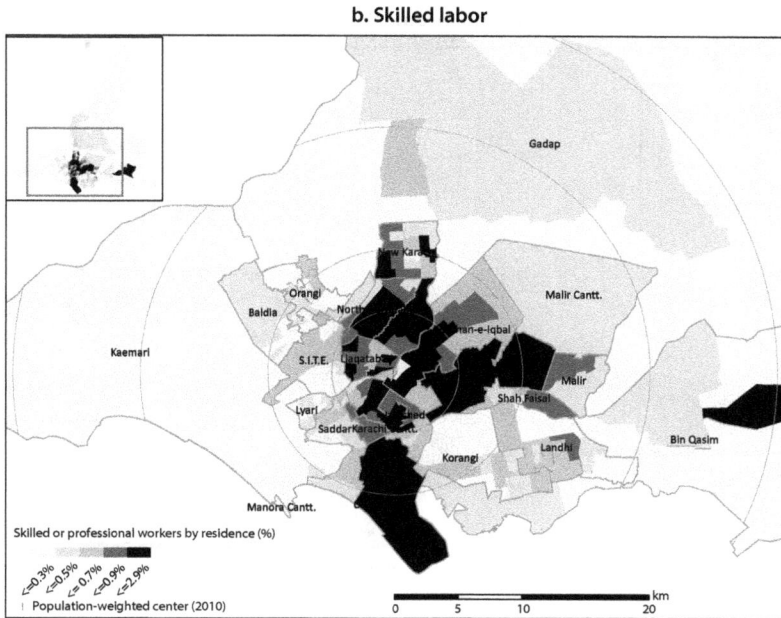

Skilled or professional workers by residence (%)

<=0.3% <=0.5% <= 0.7% <=0.9% <=2.9%

Population-weighted center (2010)

km
0   5   10   20

c. Unskilled or semiskilled labor

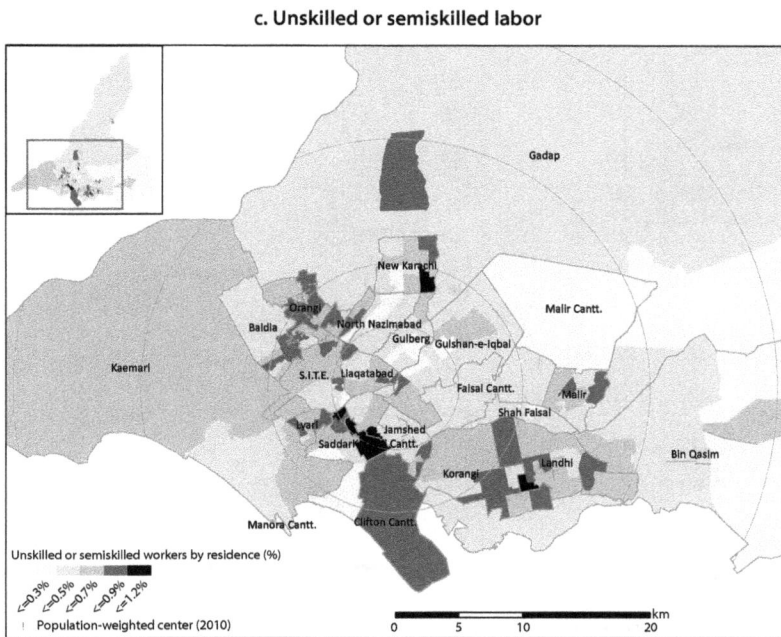

Unskilled or semiskilled workers by residence (%)

<=0.3% <=0.5% <=0.7% <=0.9% <=1.2%

Population-weighted center (2010)

km
0   5   10   20

Source: World Bank analysis, based on JICA 2010–11 Karachi Household Survey.
Note: Data at Union Council (UC) level. Panel *a* shows employment-to-residents ratio in shading and daily employment inflow in circles.

Map 3.3 Income Disparity across Karachi, Where Those with High Incomes Live around Downtown and the Unemployed Live on the Periphery and in Informal Settlements

a. High-income distribution

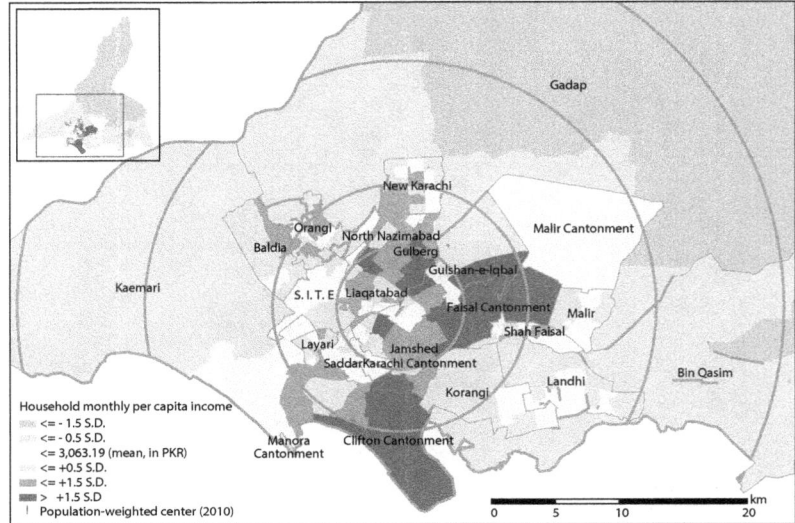

b. Unemployed distribution

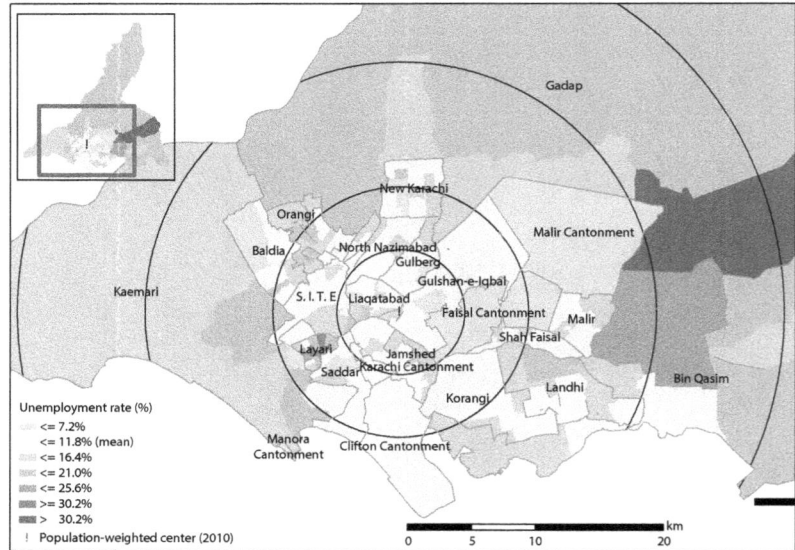

Source: World Bank analysis, based on JICA 2010–11 Karachi Household Survey.
Note: Data at Union Council (UC) level. Panel *a* shows distribution of monthly per capita income of each UC relative to average levels across all UCs. Panel *b* shows unemployment rate for each UC.

planning and service delivery, which have bolstered service-delivery "mafias." Formal services are available primarily in formally planned areas—for the most part, those developed in the 1950s and 1960s for postpartition immigrants. Military-owned or privately funded developments that proliferated in recent decades also focused on middle classes, adding a socioeconomic element to citizens' ability to access services.

Better land use, urban design, and urban transport integration are needed to serve residents and businesses and to manage congestion. Efforts to improve mass transit in Karachi must be complemented with good local area planning and urban design. For example, currently, almost all the bus rapid transit routes that are planned or under development pass through or terminate at Quaid-e-Azam's mausoleum. There is a need for a detailed urban design plan at this prominent location, which is also a gateway to the city's central commercial areas for traffic coming from the north and northeast.

Access to public recreational urban spaces for citizens is under threat. High-density developments and luxury apartments on inner city lands are also commonly perceived as displacing public spaces and recreational spaces, such as beaches, for the middle and lower classes. Public spaces, if properly designed and managed, can be pathways toward more inclusive development in a currently segregated city. The recent completion of the pedestrianized street fronting the Karachi Port Trust Building and the public space at Pakistan Chowk are welcome additions to the city.

The city has allowed its heritage assets to dilapidate. The Sindh Cultural Heritage (Preservation) Act was enacted in 1994, and a listing of heritage buildings was created. However, with the high-rise construction allowed in city core areas, especially the Old Town areas, city heritage could come under threat. New tall buildings must complement the scale and architecture of historic buildings, and dilapidated historic buildings can be put to better adaptive reuse. This displacement of people and livelihoods must be addressed in the process.

The China-Pakistan Economic Corridor (CPEC) may influence the future development of the city. Road infrastructure investments are anticipated to be worth approximately US$11 billion. A 1,100-kilometer-long freeway will be constructed between the cities of Karachi and Lahore. The expected impact of CPEC includes the following:

Trade and services. There would be an increase in economic volume, which would have an impact on the trade and service sectors, the stock exchange, the price of commodities, land development, and other activities.

Real estate, construction, and housing. The CPEC could drive real estate and housing as well as communication, transport, and construction industries.

Land use and connectivity. While it is envisaged that economic activity would spread along the CPEC, the southern bypass could see additional freight transport activities, and the northern bypass and other major arteries may expect increased traffic to serve housing and commercial uses.

Transforming Karachi into a Livable and Competitive Megacity
http://dx.doi.org/10.1596/978-1-4648-1211-8

Recommendations

1. Consolidation of accurate city data will be a first step toward effective long-term integrated planning. There is an urgent need for accurate population data and projections for planning, given the large-scale changes that have taken place since the last census, in 1998. Cities can shape more livable urban environments by planning and anticipating for the long term. Land-use and spatial planning can safeguard space for the longer term and protect the environment while responding to market demand and space needs for businesses, housing, and amenities. To reap dividends, the following are needed: better land administration; transparent development and real estate indicators, transactions, and processes; and links to the tax system.

2. Regional planning is required to reap benefits from an economic corridor. Large-scale growth is expected from the CPEC. A regional plan is needed to reap the benefits associated with such growth—and for equitable, inclusive, and efficient growth—while safeguarding environmental and cultural assets.

3. A better structure plan and a focus on implementation and development control are needed to accommodate and guide future growth. Given the population size and land area of Karachi, the city can look toward a more polycentric approach in tandem with downtown rejuvenation as a strategy to reorganize the city in a more efficient and sustainable way for the longer term. This is timely, given the planned implementation of a bus rapid transit (BRT) system that could make areas in Karachi more accessible. With the rapid changes in development, there is an opportunity to conduct a mid-term review and refine the KSDP 2020 with better frameworks to respond to challenges that have arisen since its inception in 2007. For example, Karachi could consider better distribution of jobs and housing and plans that can help facilitate private participation in urban development. Internal best practices point toward regular revision of long-term plans to respond better to city needs. These plans must translate to implementable, transparent policies that can respond to city needs and private sector development in the shorter term. (See appendix D for a case study of Singapore's planning framework.)

4. Coordination will be necessary and critical. Various land-owning agencies at different levels will need to work closely to meet the needs of the city in a coordinated and efficient way. Second, given that the public sector controls more than 90 percent of the land in Karachi Division, it is even more critical that it takes the lead in ensuring quality development for economic, social, and environmental needs. Coordination could take the form of a consultative steering committee with membership from all land-owning infrastructure agencies, stakeholders, and service providers, supported by an expert panel.

5. Land administration must be enhanced to support growth and livability. Less than 5 percent of the city's land is controlled by private entities. There are opportunities to explore appropriate, transparent mechanisms for land disposal and allocation so that land resources can better respond to demand and private-sector needs.

6. Livability and inclusion can be improved by leveraging city assets, such as heritage buildings, waterfronts, and public spaces. The impact of allowing high-rise development in Karachi, especially in the city core areas and the Clifton area, coupled with lending-rate cuts, have driven speculative activity in the housing and commercial markets. While the densification and development of the core city areas could help rejuvenate the city and create a more compact city form, high housing prices could exacerbate the exclusionary nature of urban development in Karachi. Coupled with the government of Sindh's plans for redevelopment of the *katchi abadis* through partnerships with private developers, the poor may be shifted out of the inner city. There is a need for inclusive spatial planning, such as ensuring that public amenities are accessible and open to all in these areas. See appendix D for a case study of Medellín's transformation through the implementation of inclusive public spaces). Giving special focus to the needs of women and other usually excluded and vulnerable groups in these areas will make these programs more inclusive and responsive to citizens' needs. The availability of safe public spaces for women will reduce the likelihood of harassment and violence, and help improve their participation in civic, public, and economic activities.

7. Plans to improve resilience to external shocks and climate change should be incorporated into urban planning. The recent heat wave in 2015 and the city's susceptibility to floods need to be addressed. Initiatives such as "greening" the city's public spaces could not only help reduce heat islands and reduce energy consumption but also provide breathing spaces for an increasingly dense city.

City Management, Governance, and Institutional Capacity

Institutional and Structural Changes

The main structural changes in the institutional landscape in the recent period have been the following:

> *Local government (LG) legislation and election.* In 2013, the Sindh government passed the Sindh Local Government Act, providing a framework for the reinstatement of elected LGs for the first time in the province since 2010. Municipal governance in the Karachi metropolitan region has been split between the Karachi Metropolitan Corporation (KMC) and six District Municipal Corporations (DMCs), working in overlapping geographical jurisdiction, with the mayor heading the KMC and elected chairmen heading the other entities. Rural areas are governed by the District Council. However, this law provides a multitude of powers to the provincial government, giving it strong control over the functions of the LGs and reducing their autonomy. The process for electing the mayor and chairmen was completed in August 2016, with elected leadership at the local level taking office after a period of more than five years. (See appendix J for a snapshot of the functions and responsibilities of city governments in Karachi under the prevailing LG system.)

Urban transit authority. The government of Sindh (GoS) has created the Sindh Mass Transit Authority (SMTA), and the legislature has recommended that the city's mayor should be part of its steering committee.

Development authority. In 2016, GoS restored the Karachi Development Authority (KDA) as an independent entity under its control. This entity was part of the municipal government for most of the past two decades. This has implications for Karachi's planning and development, as KDA is mandated to develop vacant land and bring it to the market.

Master planning. GoS has placed the master plan office of the city government under the provincial Sindh Building Control Authority, effectively bringing strategic city planning for Karachi under its control and unifying the functions of master planning and building control under one entity.

Other recent legislative changes that could indirectly affect planning and development in Karachi include the following:

High-density and special-development boards. GoS created the High-Density Development Board in 2010 to provide coordinated and integrated development of designated high-density zones in cities, including Karachi. In addition, it created the Special-Development Board in 2014 to facilitate low-cost housing development, rehabilitation of *katchi abadis* and slum areas, as well as multistory and high-rise development in cities. GoS controls both these boards. However, there are concerns about coordination between high-density development as mandated by the board and infrastructure and planning for the city, resulting in increased pressure on the city's services.

Public-private partnership legislation. GoS has extended the public-private partnership legal framework to include citizen organizations, with activities to include health, education, special development, and women's development. Private voluntary contributions, financial or otherwise, are also deemed acceptable.

Planning, Coordination, and Institutional Fragmentation

Implementation of the city's strategic plan was not very successful, despite the intent to coordinate planning. Karachi's planning and municipal control are highly fragmented—there are about 20 federal, provincial, and local agencies with separate legal and administrative frameworks, with little institutional coordination. (Refer to appendix E for a breakdown of land ownership and control in Karachi.) In 2007, the City District Government Karachi formulated the KSDP 2020 and approved it through a resolution passed by the city council. However, the plan did not have a binding mandate on the various provincial agencies, pending formal approval by GoS. These agencies continued to follow their independent development plans, and it has been reported that many interventions proposed in KSDP 2020 have not been implemented.

The limited success of urban management and planning is primarily due to insufficient institutional capacity, coordination, and control among land-owning agencies and the federal, provincial, and local-level authorities. This has been exacerbated by the complex political economy of the city. There are (i) fragmentation of authority over land, (ii) insufficient coordination among agencies, and (c) weak enforcement of the existing planning regulations. Nearly 90 percent of the city's land is under public ownership or control, but the owners are reluctant or unable to make this land available for development and affordable housing in a coordinated manner. The local government itself only controls about 30 percent of Karachi Division's land.[5]

The GoS strategy of centralizing the planning and building control functions at the provincial level has yet to improve coordination between Karachi's planning, service delivery, and urban management. A focus on integrated planning and service-delivery models is needed.

Limited mandates for city governments and high and increasing fragmentation in local governance prevent Karachi from reaping the benefits of urbanization. This also reduces efficiency in the planning and delivery of city services. While the KMC and six DMCs together provide various municipal functions, there is no formal coordination mechanism or relationship between them. Many municipal functions are run through GoS departments or GoS-controlled entities. This results in city governments lacking authority to deliver on municipal service mandates. Numerous entities are fully controlled by GoS: Karachi Water and Sewerage Board, Sindh Solid Waste Management Board, Sindh Building Control Authority, Karachi Development Authority, Lyari and Malir Development Authorities, Sindh Mass Transit Authority, Sindh High Density Development Board, and others. All these provide municipal or urban planning functions (table 3.1).

Table 3.1 List of Government Entities Involved in Urban Planning and Service Delivery in Karachi

Sector/area	Government agencies involved	
	Provincial	City/local
Urban planning, land use, and building control	Sindh Building Control Authority	KMC, DMCs
	Karachi, Lyari, and Malir Development Authorities	
	Sindh High-Density Development Board	
	Sindh Special-Development Board	
	Directorate of Urban Policy and Strategic Planning	
	Board of Revenue	
	Sindh Katchi Abadis Authority	
Urban transport	Transport and Mass Transit Department	KMC and DMCs in limited manner, restricted to roads, streets, parking, and some transit route permitting
Water and sewerage	Karachi Water and Sewerage Board	KMC and DMCs in limited manner, restricted to storm water drainage, etc.
Solid waste	Sindh Solid Waste Management Board	KMC and DMCs, until function taken over by SSWMB

Source: World Bank staff.
Notes: DMC = District Municipal Corporation; KMC = Karachi Metropolitan Corporation; SSWMB = Sindh Solid Waste Management Board.

Recommendations

1. Holding LG elections is only the beginning of the journey toward better services. The government of Pakistan needs to do more to address deficits of local government:

   Empower local government. Overall, functions and resources assigned to LGs in Pakistan are very limited, and Karachi is no exception. An elected, empowered, and inclusive city government in Karachi is essential for improving the physical and social environment of the city.

   Enhance accountability mechanisms for upward and downward accountability. Elections are critical to any local accountability system, but not sufficient in and of themselves. An LG system needs appropriate upward reporting and accountability mechanisms (to higher levels of government) to ensure consistency and transparency of administration, management, and oversight. Equally important are provisions for downward accountability mechanisms (to citizens), electoral and nonelectoral, that create spaces for citizens to place demands on elected LG officials and local bureaucracies and help create more inclusive city governments.

2. Successfully delivering public services to citizens in the new LG system will also depend on the capacity of local officials. Instituting such capacity simultaneously in numerous local entities will be a huge challenge for GoS and will require hard work and concerted and sustained support. The current laws and regulations also need to be continuously adjusted to respond to emerging issues and situations. An ambitious program is needed to enhance the capacity of elected and appointed LG officials in delivering on their mandates.

3. Creating a platform for integrated and coordinated planning is now more critical than ever. Karachi is at a tipping point of unsustainable urban development—there are signs of serious urban sprawl, with the city core being locked into inefficient land use that will be costly to reverse. This outcome is partially because of land contestation and an uncoordinated development program among agencies across government that control land. Federal agencies such as railways, ports, and the military cantonments and DHA control more than 10 percent of the land and have their own development and planning programs, building bylaws, and zoning, with little formal coordination with the provincial or local government. (See appendix E for a breakdown of land ownership.)

4. An important step may be creating an empowered master plan office as an independent body with representation from all local governments and land-owning agencies in the city as well as civil society and technocrats. This office should bring together these entities on a formalized platform. This will help reduce the current discretionary and overriding power of GoS in land allocation decisions, especially in the city's periphery. This body may also seek to revise and update the KSDP 2020 in an inclusive manner, and obtain formal approval from GoS to give it legal backing and binding effect.

5. It is critical to create a formal mechanism for regular coordination between the two layers of Karachi's urban management working in the same jurisdiction. Karachi's urban management will now be split between the KMC and six DMCs, with jurisdictional and functional overlap between the two layers. The LG model in the metropolitan cities of Turkey is worth studying and replicating in Karachi; a highly empowered metropolitan municipality headed by an elected mayor of the large city is the overall responsible entity for planning, development, and service delivery, with a number of district municipalities as the second tier of metropolitan governance responsible for various functions.

6. The process of integrated and coordinated planning, with representation from all relevant agencies, can be made more inclusive and representative by ensuring that women and usually excluded and vulnerable groups are adequately represented in consultations with citizens, so that any updating of Karachi's strategic development plan or any investment in the city's infrastructure and services responds to the needs of these vulnerable groups.

Municipal Service Delivery and Living Standards

Providing safe, reliable, and cost-effective urban infrastructure and basic services is an important contributor to raising living standards, thereby improving quality of life. During the past two decades, Karachi has undergone infrastructure neglect and setbacks and, therefore, effort is being made to ensure the infrastructural development in the city fits its status.

Urban growth in the past two decades in the Karachi megacity has not been effectively managed or coordinated, which has forced reactive and uncoordinated public investment in infrastructure. The result has been ineffective and largely unsustainable urban development. Urban sprawl, with informal and formal development along the city's periphery, has placed immense strain on the province's and city's finances by requiring new bulk and link infrastructure extensions. The replacement, rehabilitation, and preventive maintenance of existing infrastructure have suffered because of the persistent focus on the (often reactive) extension of infrastructure, and have also been limited by budget shifts to cover other prioritized expenditure. There is thus an urgent need to raise investment levels for remedial work, upgrading, and replacement of the city's aging municipal services infrastructure.

This section looks at three critical areas of municipal infrastructure and services in Karachi: (i) urban transport, (ii) water supply and sanitation, and (iii) solid waste management.

Urban Transport

Policy and Institutional Framework

No sector-specific policy exists for urban transport in Karachi. While several studies have been completed, a coherent and holistic policy was never formulated.

Transforming Karachi into a Livable and Competitive Megacity
http://dx.doi.org/10.1596/978-1-4648-1211-8

Most recently, a comprehensive study was undertaken to draft a sustainable urban transport policy for Sindh, financed through the Pakistan Sustainable Transport Project, funded by the Global Environment Facility and the United Nations Development Program.

Multiple government departments and authorities are dealing with transport in the city and have no coordination among them. Various bodies—such as the National Highway Authority, GoS, KMC, DHA, and cantonments—administer roads in Karachi. The KMC is responsible for the administration of over 40 percent of roads in the city. The Transport and Mass Transit Department is the principal planning, regulatory, and implementing body of GoS responsible for dealing with all urban transport matters at the provincial level. Currently, responsibilities for major roads transport and traffic management within the city are shared between two departments of the KMC—Work and Services as well as Transport and Communications.

Fares for public transport are regulated by the GoS Transport and Mass Transit Department. The District Regional Transport Authority (DRTA) issues route permission for public transport in Karachi. However, the decision making for the permission is governed by a board, with representation from the police, city government, and Provincial Transport Authority and DRTA. The public-private partnership (PPP) unit of the GoS is also assisting the Transport and Mass Transport Department in the development of mass transit initiatives in Karachi.

Sector Structure and Assets Ownership

Citizens rely almost entirely on the road network for urban transportation. The city has approximately 10,000 kilometers of roads, with local roads accounting for 93 percent and highways and arterial roads for less than 5 percent of the total length. Karachi has also six arterial or trunk roads that extend radially from the central area.

There is currently no mass transit system per se, although many people commute via the network of bus routes. There are nearly 13.5 million mechanized trips made each day within the city, of which about 42 percent are made by public and 58 percent by private transport. There were 3.6 million registered vehicles in Karachi as of mid-2015 (over 30 percent of the national total), and private vehicles—mainly motorcycles and cars—constitute about 84 percent of total registered vehicles, while public transport accounts for 4.5 percent of the total registered vehicles. With growth rates for private vehicles at over 4 percent, there are now over 1,000 new vehicles added to the streets of the city each day.

Buses, minibuses, coaches, and vans are the major transport modes in Karachi. There are over 12,000 buses, minibuses, and coaches plying 267 routes in the city. The bus fleet has been decreasing in size without any other mode to adequately replace it. The number of minibuses has declined from around 22,000 in 2010–11 to the current total of around 9,500.

Sector Performance and Main Issues

The main causes of the failure of urban transport in Karachi are the absence of a cohesive government policy and strategy, and the lack of a clear decision-making structure. Karachi's urban transport has suffered from frequent regulatory and institutional changes, preventing planning for and implementing of a holistic and integrated urban transport system. Matters are further compounded by the involvement of several federal, provincial, and local bodies and a lack of coordination among these stakeholders.

Public transport, which constitutes about 5 percent of the number of vehicles on roads, carries 42 percent of travelers. Private cars carry 21 percent, and motorcycles 19 percent of the traveling public. This means that cars and motorcycles, which account for 84 percent of the vehicles on roads, carry only 40 percent of commuters. The number of passengers competing for a single bus seat in Karachi is 45, which is one of the highest in the world. In comparison, 12 people compete for a single bus seat in Mumbai, and only 8 in Hong Kong, China.

The large gap between demand and supply has resulted in a proliferation of other transport modes, with demand shifting from buses to rickshaws, Suzuki pickups, and *chingchis* and an increasing number of private cars and motorbikes.[6] Consequently, traffic congestion has become a critical issue in Karachi, which brings about environmental problems and a loss of productivity. The traffic congestion causes low fuel efficiency, another problem of the transport system in Karachi.

Trips made by private vehicles (motorcycles, cars, and so forth) account for 53 percent of the total mechanized trips being generated. At the same time, the average volume-to-capacity road traffic ratio is 1.1, which indicates that on average, 110 percent of the total capacity of the roads is utilized (that is, slightly exceeding their capacity). In short, the majority of trips are made via private vehicle, and the roads are overcrowded.

Of all trips (both mechanized and nonmechanized), walking is the most predominant form of travel, with 46 percent of trips made by foot, compared to 11 percent by cars.[7]

Transport-related problems have increased in recent decades in Karachi. They include (i) traffic congestion contributing to increased air and noise pollution, leading to health problems; (ii) high accident rates; and (iii) environmental degradation. These problems contribute to declining living standards, long commutes, and limits on people's livelihood choices, determining to a significant degree where they live, which in turn worsens congestion. These, in turn, relate to drops in income and a decrease in personal security, which have affected the most vulnerable groups.

Women are the worst affected by the transport crisis. Many women do not work as a result; and the decisions of those who do, and the jobs they opt for, depend very much on the availability of transport.

The main issues facing the transport sector in Karachi can be summarized as follows:

Complex institutional and organizational structure. The urban transport sector in Karachi faces a typical administrative problem between a strong megacity and its higher state government. The complex relation between the city government and GoS is one of the reasons for the slow implementation of BRT projects. The Karachi Mass Transit Cell in the city government was the responsible agency for mass transit development and was engaged in bidding for priority corridor construction and a compressed natural gas bus project. However, it has not been given enough authority over project financing, contracts for operation and maintenance, control and enforcement over operators, and other essential powers for the implementation of a mass transit system. The cell is now being converted to the SMTA at the provincial level.

Low capacity of bus service. Most megacities in developing countries suffer from a large number of small buses (minibuses) that cause serious congestion in the city centers, especially in the absence of a mass transit system. Usually, the introduction of a mass transit system can be justified from the huge demand for public transport in these cities. However, public transport in Karachi is fast deteriorating, with the number of buses decreasing and traffic demand increasing with rapid population growth, city expansion, and economic growth. Currently, there is a shortage of close to 8,000 buses, which will just cover the immediate demand.

Improper bus routes and poor road networks. The majority of the bus services concentrate on radial directions, and there is no route hierarchy in the bus network or the trunk and feeder system. Most of the local road network is not in a good condition, especially in more populated districts and poor neighborhoods.

Traffic congestion. Traffic congestion is a serious problem, especially in the center of the city. A lot of traffic signals are installed at intersections in the central city area compared to the suburban area. However, in peak hours police control traffic because of the problems of the signalized intersections.

Lack of parking spaces. While common to many large cities, for Karachi this is a major issue. The capacity of public parking is very small compared to the demand. In most of the commercial areas, parking spaces are also heavily encroached upon by vendor carts and stalls. Double parking and illegal parking are common in the main business districts, which causes serious traffic congestion.

Recommendations

Technical measures alone are unlikely to resolve the fundamental paradox of the Karachi transport sector—combining excess demand with inadequately financed and managed supply. There is no doubt that improvements in the efficiency of roads, vehicles, public transport operations, and traffic management can improve urban transport service delivery in Karachi. What is urgently required is an integrated package of policy measures founded in well-designed and well-functioning institutions within an appropriate political framework.

There are no easy or quick-fix solutions, and a phased approach can be adopted to tackle the critical challenges and issues toward gradual improvements of the economic, financial, and social performance of the transport service systems in Karachi.

Short Term

1. Improve the governance and institutional structure. Karachi's transport problems cannot be resolved by improving infrastructure or the provision of public transport facilities alone. The solution lies in adopting a comprehensive strategy and efficient institutions that have buy-in from all major stakeholders. Most of the larger cities of the world are responsible for urban transport planning and implementation. The setting-up of the SMTA could be a step in the right direction, but its success will depend on (i) sustainability and (ii) inclusion of the stakeholders. To do this, it is important that the SMTA has ample representation from the city government.
2. Improve the management of existing urban road space. Simply expanding road infrastructure to keep pace with high vehicle growth will not work. The short-term measures could include (i) enhancing traffic management (recirculation, channelization, and centralized traffic signaling); (b) providing off-street parking; and (c) improving enforcement, via public awareness and citizen support.
3. Improve the nonmotorized transport environment. Ensure that facilities for pedestrians are cared for—sidewalks, road crossings, bikeways, and so forth. The focus should be to incentivize walking travelers to shift to public rather than private transport.
4. Implement an intelligent transport system that uses cameras and sensors for traffic counts and emission monitoring. Generate open data and encourage innovation (such as apps development).
5. Conduct traffic safety audits. Traffic safety has become a serious concern, with some 983 road accidents reported in 2013 (of which 615 were fatal). Vulnerable pedestrian road users constitute the largest proportion of traffic fatalities, primarily due to inadequate pedestrian walkways and cycle routes. The city's Transport Department should conduct a traffic safety audit to identify major danger spots. Some of these can be improved with a very small investment and with minor improvement to traffic flow.
6. Rationalize the route system. Public transport route rationalization has not been done since the mid-1980s, whereas the city continues to expand and usage patterns continue to change. There is a need to immediately undertake a route rationalization study. In the short term this will help in optimizing the existing bus and minibus fleet.
7. Change building-control regulations. Mandating a traffic impact assessment to be conducted for all new multistory buildings would be a significant help.

Medium to Long Terms

1. Large investments are needed to close the city's gaps in terms of urban transport infrastructure. The total investment needs over the upcoming 10 years are estimated at PRs 550 billion (US$5.5 billion). However, while substantial requirements can be met through public-sector spending, unless private-sector financing is tapped, the ambitious investment agenda will be difficult to fulfill. Mass transit systems appear to yield the greatest benefit when they are incorporated into a citywide price-level and structure plan, in which the effects of the full cost of new mass transit investments on the province and city budgets, on fares, and on poor people have been estimated in advance.

2. There is a need to include a sizable bus fleet in the system. However, rather than the government procuring and running the new buses, the right enabling environment should be created for private-sector participation. Efforts should also be made to provide incentives for the existing bus and minibus owners and operators to organize themselves into more formal associations or companies, with easier access to financing for fleet replacement and modernization.

3. Undertaking a massive program of setting up a modern public transport system also requires substantial capacity building of the appropriate transport and mass transit departments, at both the provincial and city government levels. This should include capacity not only in terms of planning, implementing, and operating large public transport systems but also in managing PPP transactions.

4. Making public transport systems safe and reliable for women and vulnerable groups is key. Although they travel less frequently, women, the elderly, and other vulnerable groups are disproportionately higher users of public transport than men—since men often use motorbikes for nonwalking trips, which these groups do not, due to social norms.[8] Women face substantial challenges while using public transport due to harassment and social norms. Thus, investments to make public transport safe, reliable, and affordable for them are of critical importance. These interventions will increase women's opportunities to access jobs, education, and civic opportunities and help mitigate the impact of social norms.

Water Supply and Sanitation

Policy and Institutional Framework

National policies relevant to water supply and wastewater services in Karachi include the National Water Policy, the National Drinking Water Policy, and the National Sanitation Policy. The overall goals of the National Drinking Water Policy are to (i) ensure safe drinking water to the entire population at an affordable cost in an equitable, efficient, and sustainable manner; and (ii) ensure reduction in the incidence of mortality and morbidity caused by waterborne diseases.

Neither the province nor the city has a formal policy for the WSS sector. In the absence of such a framework, fiscal support to the Karachi Water and Sewerage Board (KWSB) has been ad hoc and often aimed at addressing its immediate financial difficulties rather than funding longer-term goals or transformation. A provincial drinking water policy is, however, under preparation. The 2008 JICA-funded study of the water supply and sewerage system in Karachi remains the most recent overview of infrastructure needs and planning for the city's WSS sector, but limited planned interventions have been undertaken.

The provision of WSS in Karachi is the primary responsibility of KWSB. After passing through various institutional transformations, KWSB was created in 1983 as a single water utility within the KMC, responsible for planning, development, management, and revenue collection related to water and sanitation services. In 1996, KWSB was separated from the KMC and was put under the administrative control of the Local Government Department of GoS. The legal framework, specification of functions, relevant financial guidelines, and delegation of powers were provided in KWSB Act 1996, including production, transmission, and distribution; cost recovery of potable water; management of the sewerage system; development of schemes to cover shortfalls in services; and collection of revenues. KWSB currently has about 13,500 employees and had an estimated budget for 2014–15 of US$222 million.

However, de facto, KWSB enjoys only very limited autonomy. Key functions—including approval of budgets, regulations and tariffs, hiring and postings, and provision or facilitation of locally mobilized funds or foreign loans or grants—lie within the purview of the provincial government. Additionally, KWSB relies directly on subsidies from the provincial government and is fully dependent on provincial and federal funds for debt servicing and infrastructure expansion to meet growing needs and close the service deficit gap. In 2014, it received a US$50 million subsidy toward payment of electricity bills to Karachi Electric.[9] The current payable debts of KWSB to Karachi Electric are around US$320 million.

Sector Structure and Assets Ownership

Water supply is a significant challenge facing Karachi, with only 55 percent of water requirements being currently met. Per design, Karachi receives an inflow of 650 million gallons per day (MGD), mainly from two sources: the Indus River to the east of the city and the Hub Dam, a large water-storage reservoir constructed in 1981 on the Hub River, which flows west of the city. The Hub reservoir was not able to supply water for several years in the late 1990s and early 2000s, as the dam's catchment area was dry during the monsoon season. As per the World Health Organization's standard of 55 gallons per capita per day, Karachi's current water needs are estimated at 1,200 MGD. This translates into a shortfall of more than 550 MGD. According to KSDP 2020 estimates, the need is expected to reach 1,400 MGD by 2020.

KWSB owns and manages public water supply and sewerage systems. Karachi's water supply infrastructure comprises 150 pumping stations, 25 bulk water reservoirs, 8 water-filtration plants, 20 sewage-pumping stations, over 11,000 kilometers of pipeline, 75 kilometers of canals, 3 sewage treatment plants, and over 250,000 manholes. KWSB provides water supply and sewerage services to Karachi through 1.13 million domestic connections and 9,317 bulk customers.[10]Approximately 250,000 customers are being served by KWSB indirectly through bulk connections. A further 2.05 million units or customers are also served by KWSB directly.

Nonpiped systems, including private water tankers, are abundant and form the major source of domestic water supply in Karachi, particularly in informal settlements. KWSB has 24 hydrants licensed to private parties, of which 10 are operational and the remainder were closed as per a recent Supreme Court Order. The construction of illegal hydrants is widespread. In an effort to control illegal water tapping, KWSB introduced amendments to discourage illegal hydrants and has dismantled 948 illegal hydrants since 2009. In 2015, 10 KWSB hydrants were metered. However, only three metered hydrants are currently operational. On average, 20 MGD water is supplied from 24 hydrants providing water to underserved populations, mostly low-income households.

Access and Quality of Service

Water supply in Karachi is highly irregular and inequitable. Data show that access to improved water sources has declined in the past 10 years in Karachi, slipping from 90 percent coverage of the population in 2006–07 to 86 percent in 2014–15 (figure 3.3). Further, rationing of water supply is widespread in most places, particularly in poor neighborhoods. More than 50 percent of Karachi's population lives in informal settlements, and most of them face severe shortages of water and a lack of proper sewerage systems (ADB 2007). Water availability often ranges from two hours every two days to four hours per day at very low pressure. Due to the lack of alternatives—as groundwater is brackish and KWSB is the only service provider—many households also rely

Figure 3.3 Percentage of Karachi's Population with Access to Drinking Water from Improved Sources

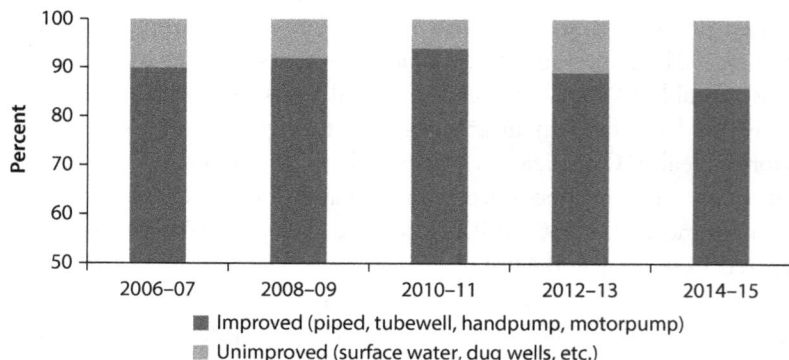

Source: Pakistan Social and Living Standards Measurements Survey and World Bank staff calculations.

on vendors that supply water through commercial tankers at high prices, especially in the summer.

A large amount of water does not reach users. The water distribution system in Karachi is, on average, about 40–45 years old, with many corroded pipes that disrupt effective transmission. It is estimated—in the absence of bulk and domestic metering—that nonrevenue water (NRW) is 35 percent (192 MGD), which includes both physical and commercial losses (leakages and large-scale, unauthorized diversion or thefts). This figure could increase to 285 MGD after completion of the K-IV Phase I project (which will bring an additional 260 MGD water) if NRW is left unattended. In the absence of bulk and consumer (domestic and commercial) metering, the likelihood is that NRW is significantly higher than what KWSB estimates. Table 3.2 presents the revenue losses. This means that KWSB is recovering revenue only for 337 MGD, relative to a total supply of 550 MGD, which puts the revenue loss at 43 percent (237 MGD).

NRW can be attributed to the absence of domestic meters; the fact that the distribution network is old and rusty, with poor workmanship causing leaking joints; and a culture of postponing routine maintenance due to a lack of finances. In the absence of domestic metering, calculation of physical losses (losses in the distribution network) is difficult, but a conservative estimate of combined NRW from physical and commercial losses is around 55–60 percent.

Access to and the cost of water are acute problems for women, who are often the sole caretakers of the household and children. Women living in communities with poor access to clean water either must (i) revert to carrying dirty and contaminated water from a well or from a river or canal that ends up endangering the lives of their families or (ii) buy water from private tankers, despite unsure availability and the water's exorbitant cost, which is onerous given meager household incomes. In many cases, the water provided

Table 3.2 Estimation of Nonrevenue Water (Commercial Losses) in Karachi, FY2014–15

	Bulk	Hydrants	Retail (total metered flow)	Total
		Total inflow 550 MGD		Total
Inflow (MGD)	130[a]	20[a]	400	550
Number of consumers	9,317	24	1,716,140	1,725,481
Consumers billed	9,317	24	1,716,140	1,725,481
Amount billed (US$ millions)	59.03	16.6[b]	34.9	110.53
Amount collected (US$ millions)	36.6	16.6	18.75	71.95
Collection efficiency (%)	62	100	53	72
Revenue loss (US$ millions)	22.43	0	16.15	38.58
Revenue loss (flow MGD)	49.4	0	188	237.4
Revenue water (MGD)	100.6	24	212	336.6

Source: World Bank analysis based on primary data collected from KWSB.
a. Metered supply.
b. Legal hydrants amount billed, calculated using tariff of PRs 237 per 1,000 gallons.

through tankers is of poor quality and increases the risk of diseases, especially among children.

More than 6 million Karachiites have no access to public sewerage service. Sewerage network coverage is estimated at 60 percent and faces complex challenges of inadequate sewer trunk mains, malfunctioning pumping facilities, and insufficient wastewater treatment capacity.

The amount of raw sewage discharged into the sea each day is 475 MGD. The sewerage network of the city has had very little maintenance since the 1960s (ADB 2007), and the three existing wastewater treatment plants are dysfunctional. Additionally, separation of municipal wastewater from industrial effluent is not a common practice. Two of the biggest industrial estates in Pakistan, both located in Karachi, have no effluent treatment plant, and the waste—containing hazardous materials, heavy metals, oil, and so on—is discharged into Karachi's rivers and the already polluted harbor (Worldwide Fund for Nature 2007).

Efficiency and Sustainability

The existing water and sanitation systems in Karachi underperform on most international standards for efficient and sustainable service delivery. The operational inefficiencies of KWSB—including revenue undercollection, distribution losses, and labor inefficiencies—cost the province millions of dollars every year.

Collection efficiency of KWSB is far below global best practices. Operating inefficiencies are divided between revenue undercollection and distribution losses. KWSB has a computerized monthly billing cycle. On average, it generates PRs 850 million (US$8.5 million) per month, while it collects PRs 550 million (US$5.5 million) per month, which puts collection efficiency at around 65 percent, far below the best practice of 100 percent (table 3.3 and figure 3.4). Average distribution and transmission losses in Karachi are 35 percent, far above the norm of 20 percent.

Poor billing and collection efficiency and the nature of the tariff structure also inhibit efforts to bridge the receipts-expenditure gap. Only 30 percent, or 300,000 out of a total 1.1 million customers, are being billed. The revenue collection decreased from 61 percent to 59 percent during the past five years

Table 3.3 KWSB's Revenue Collection Efficiency

Bill demand generated	Collection efficiency (%)			
		Bulk consumers		
Year	Retail domestic	Domestic	Commercial/industrial	Total
2010–11	58.4	57.3	72.2	61.3
2011–12	48.4	58.7	74.8	58.5
2012–13	46.0	64.1	76.6	60.4
2013–14	59.7	57.9	75.6	63.8
2014–15	53.6	51.6	72.9	58.9
2015–16 (7 months)	52.8	36.3	77.8	55.4

Source: World Bank analysis, based on primary data collected from KWSB.

Figure 3.4 KWSB's Revenues and Major Expenditure Items

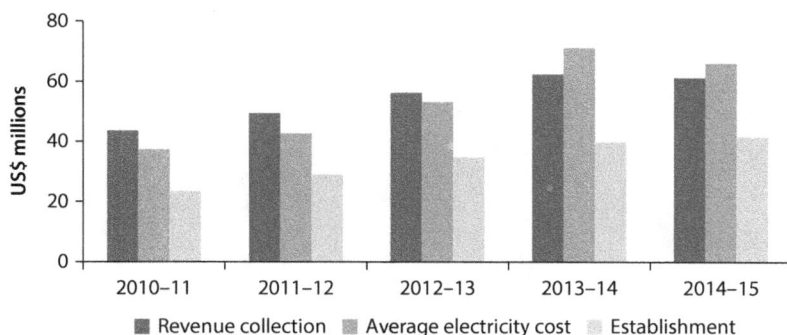

Source: World Bank analysis, based on primary data collected from KWSB.

Table 3.4 Analysis of KWSB's Water Tariffs

Customer type	Charging basis	Tariff (PRs per 1,000 gallons)	Cost of production (PRs per 1,000 gallons)	Subsidy (PRs per 1,000 gallons)
Bulk-metered domestic	Volumetric	130	286	156
Bulk-metered industrial	Volumetric	222	286	64
Bulk-metered commercial	Volumetric	222	286	64
Domestic (unmetered)	Plot size/flat rate	100[a]	286	186
Hydrants	Volumetric	237	286	49

Source: World Bank analysis, based on primary data collected from KWSB.
a. Cost and consumption of water calculated for sampled plot size (401–600 square yards), assuming per capita consumption of 40 gallons per capita per day and household size of 5.5 persons per household.

(table 3.4). It is estimated that less than half of the registered 1.04 million consumers pay their monthly water bills. The total outstanding arrears are estimated at US$460 million (US$179 million for retail and US$281 million for bulk) and continue to accumulate. Government institutions and utilities are among the largest defaulters, owing the equivalent of US$350 million to KWSB.

In Karachi, retail-level water supply is not metered, and consumers are billed on flat rates based on size of plots. Only 25 percent of the industrial or commercial customers have metered supply, with the remainder billed on connection size. Domestic connections are not metered, and tariffs are thus based on property size and not on volumetric consumption. The average water tariff is low, at US$0.13 per cubic meter, which creates a disincentive for any form of water savings (table 3.4). Additionally, there are no charges for sewerage services.

Additionally, KWSB suffers from overstaffing and labor inefficiency. It has around 13,500 employees, or 6.5 employees per 1,000 connections, more than twice the 2.0 employees per 1,000 connections frequently used as the international benchmark for developing countries. Along with electricity charges, salaries and benefits (establishment cost) represent about 92 percent of the total expenditures of KWSB. This situation leaves very

Figure 3.5 Trends in KWSB Expenditure from 2010 to 2015

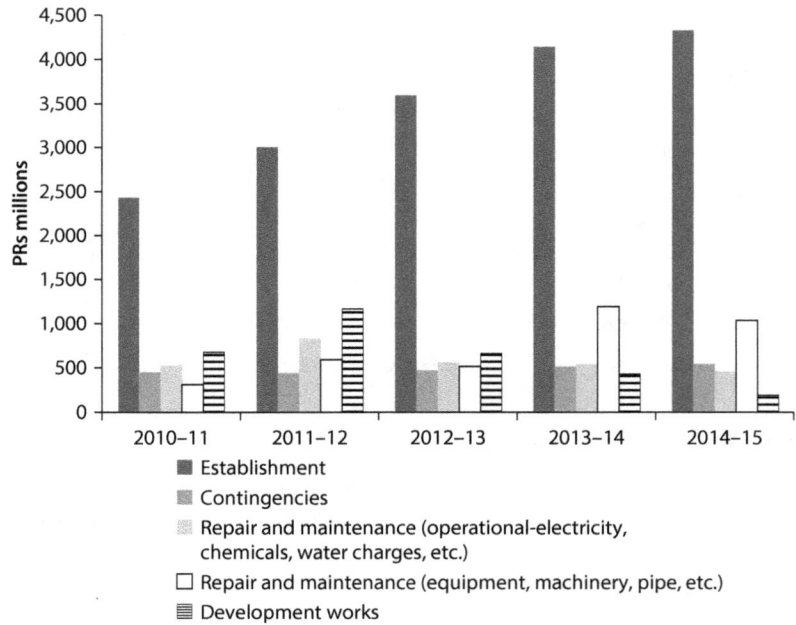

Source: World Bank analysis, based on primary data collected from KWSB.

little fiscal space for KWSB to invest and carry out regular operation and maintenance of its assets. KWSB management must often choose among paying salaries, buying fuel, or purchasing spare parts, and defaulting on the electricity bill (figure 3.5).

Investment Trends and Future Needs

Over the past 10 years, capital expenditures in the water and sanitation sector totaled over US$65 million. The vast majority of this investment was undertaken with the support of the provincial and federal governments. The amount of investment has been decreasing since 2008 (figure 3.6). The investment level is insufficient to close the current gap in terms of access and quality and to keeping pace with growing demand and service targets.

Additionally, the actual investment amount is far from the estimated investment requirements for water supply to ensure universal access to safe and affordable drinking water by 2030, one of the Sustainable Development Goals. In 2007, the JICA WSS Master Plan for Karachi estimated the total investment needs for both WSS at US$2.6 billion (2008–25).

Karachi's water and sewerage crisis is foremost a governance and institutional one. Without a viable governance framework that clearly delineates the appropriate roles and responsibilities of relevant stakeholders in policy making, service delivery, and regulation, the long-term effects of technical, financial, or internal

Figure 3.6 Trend of Investment in Water and Sewerage in Karachi

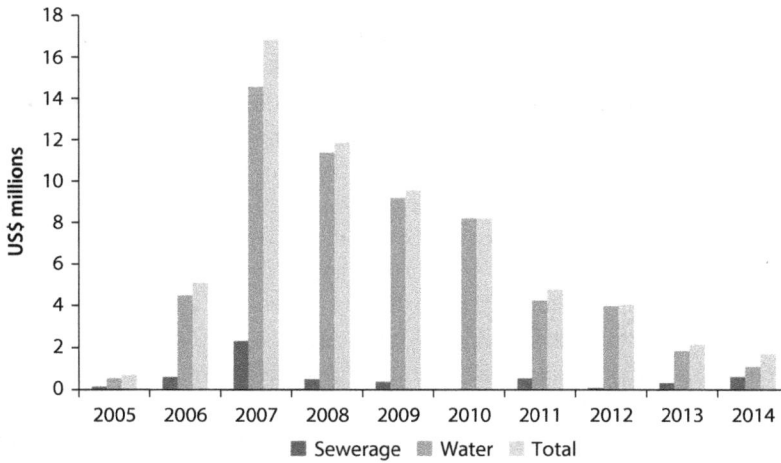

Source: World Bank analysis, based on primary data collected from KWSB.

management changes cannot be secured. While investments in infrastructure have to date lagged behind the established need, it is critical that any investment be leveraged against a significant paradigm shift to change the focus from asset creation to service delivery by addressing institutional, governance, and accountability aspects of service delivery.

Recommendations

There is a strong need to transform KWSB into a modern utility. It must be able to provide the full range of water supply and wastewater services to all users, in line with international best practices. The turnaround of a public utility such as KWSB requires a complex set of interdependent actions needing support from a range of stakeholders, including politicians, staff and managers of the utility, and the public. KWSB is aligned with the provincial government (under the 1996 KWSB Act), while utilities in other large cities in Pakistan (Lahore, Faisalabad, and Peshawar) and elsewhere in the world are either aligned with cities or are operating as autonomous public utilities. GoS needs to realign KWSB with the city government as an effective, efficient, and autonomous utility.

Karachi will need a mix of investment and supportive policy reforms to close its infrastructure gap. Moving ahead, major challenges will include prioritizing investment needs and choosing optimal forms of service provision, including the private sector's role, and clearly defining the functions and powers of institutions.

The following short-, medium-, and long-term elements are needed to address the critical institutional and governance weaknesses, inefficient operations, outdated infrastructure, and severe financial constraints.

Transforming Karachi into a Livable and Competitive Megacity
http://dx.doi.org/10.1596/978-1-4648-1211-8

Short Term
1. Transform KWSB into a modern utility. GoS needs to revisit KWSB's institutional and governance structure in the light of the enabling environment in which KWSB has been operating, its service-delivery performance, present challenges, and national and global models of utilities that have evolved in the past few years. A utility that is autonomous in its day-to-day affairs, is professionally managed by qualified staff, has a clear line of accountability, and focuses on customers has a much higher chance of delivering services than the present governance arrangement. One such example of utility reform is in Peshawar, where the World Bank supported "functional amalgamation" to transform seven municipalities into one citywide corporate utility (see appendix F). A restructured KWSB must assess its baseline performance and benchmark against similar utilities in a targeted effort to set a specific strategy for short- and medium-term service improvement. Specific components of a new KWSB strategy would include performance standards, capital investment needs, systems, procedure and equipment needs, training needs, institutional optimization, and staff and management incentive structures.
2. Improve the operating environment within KWSB. This action focuses on revising the governance structures within KWSB as well as its compact with users, both public and private. The action begins with an assessment of the institutional, regulatory, and political environment in which the utility operates and the key bottlenecks that constrain the performance of the utility. Specific actions to be implemented include (i) restructuring the KWSB board, (ii) establishing a pro-poor unit and developing a pro-poor strategy, and (iii) appointing an NRW team and associated NRW reduction strategy.
3. Revisit financial sustainability arrangements with provincial and municipal partners. Based on findings of the KWSB strategy (see first recommendation), clarify the financial relationship and interaction among all parties affected by KWSB, including financial flows toward the development of a financial stabilization plan. The analysis will cover both operating and capital costs and would allow the utility and municipality or province to explore a range of options going forward in relation to subsidies, performance improvements, tariff reforms, and so on.
4. Improve consultation and outreach with stakeholders to create meaningful citizen engagement. Reform of a public utility requires extensive consultation with a range of stakeholders—consumers, staff, managers, politicians, and nongovernmental organizations. Specific actions would include the development of a communications strategy and regular consultation and feedback to develop a turnaround package that has broad support and can be monitored in its implementation. Establishing mechanisms for redressing grievances and investing in improved customer relations would also be key to success.
5. Establish "net demand" for water. Net demand for water is the volume of water needed if NRW levels are reduced to international best practice standards for a metropolis similar to Karachi in size and context. KWSB currently lacks the appropriate management and technical expertise necessary to carry out an

effective NRW program. Specific actions in this regard would include the following: (i) customer surveys to update the customer register, (ii) identification of ring-fenced hydraulic zones for pilot NRW programs, (iii) leak detection and repair, (iv) replacement of the rusty and leaking distribution network, (v) introduction of household water metering and consumption-based tariffs, (vi) detection of illegal connections, (vii) formulation of a target-based action plan for revenue recovery, and (viii) development of a strategy to recover arrears and write off amounts that cannot be collected. The World Bank–supported Performance-Based Contract (PBC) for Reducing NRW Ho Chi Minh City (HCMC) from 2008 to 2013 is considered a globally successful NRW model (see appendix F). The current support of the World Bank Public-Private Infrastructure Advisory Facility to develop a PBC framework for NRW reduction in the Faisalabad Water and Sanitation Agency (F-WASA) offers lot of learning and localizing in the KWSB context. Urgent action is also needed to meter large, bulk-water supply consumers, including all KWSB-owned and -operated hydrants, in order to assess the volume of water being distributed through hydrants.

6. Formulate long-term sector policy and set up accountability arrangements. An inclusive mission, vision, strategy, and policy formulation exercise is required to set the direction of the sector. A comprehensive and long-term sector policy is required to outline how GoS will support KWSB in achieving its vision and how KWSB will evolve to plan and deliver services in the light of challenges. There is also a need to establish upward (through a sector regulator) and downward (through citizen engagement) accountability.

Medium Term

1. Improve pumping efficiency and rehabilitate works. KWSB's pumping stations are operating below capacity. There are no backup pumps, and available pumps are operating on a 24-hour basis. The efficiency of the pumps needs to be enhanced, pumping capacity needs to be enhanced, and backup pumps are required.

2. Improve levels of pro-poor service. Priority actions would include implementation of pro-poor strategy (developed under the first short-term recommendation) that focuses on improving service delivery for the almost 8 million residents of Karachi residing in informal communities. The strategy would address the shortfalls in water and sanitation services and examine cost-recovery models.

3. Finance an investment program that prioritizes network rehabilitation and sewerage expansion. Priority investments would include (i) replacement and/or rehabilitation of 685 kilometers of trunk mains, 9,179 kilometers of distribution network, and large pumping stations; and (ii) investment in the Sewerage: S-III Phase II–Malir Basin-Sewerage Project, which would comprise sewerage network improvements, rehabilitation of an existing treatment plant, and construction work on a treatment plant for the Malir Basin to treat 50 MGD of sewage.

Long Term

1. Finance a long-term investment program that prioritizes water transfer and distribution and short- to medium-term underpinnings for institutional and governance reforms. Future programmatic investments may include the subsequent phases of the K-IV water transfer investments and the expansion and rehabilitation of eight large filtration plans.

Municipal Solid Waste

Policy and Institutional Framework

The following assessment and recommendations were conducted soon after a new Sindh Solid Waste Management Board (SSWMB) was established in 2014 with the aim to minimize duplication of effort, optimize capacity, achieve economies of scale, and address the complicated needs for land acquisition for solid waste sites.[11] There is also a related new act for environmental projection. The new SSWMB will have full overarching authority and responsibility for waste collection, transfer, disposal, and treatment. The board has broad representation from various agencies and the private sector.[12]

It is unclear if the model of having the solid waste management function transferred from the local government to the provincial level will be sustainable in the longer term, but for the purposes of this report, it is assumed that solid waste management will be the responsibility of the province. Irrespective of the management model that the city intends to adopt, the report's technical recommendations, other than those that pertain specifically to SSWMB, remain relevant.

The responsibilities and authority granted to the board are comprehensive. They include (i) developing a tariff structure, (ii) collecting fees, (iii) managing finances, (iv) making rules and regulation, (v) monitoring waste sources, (vi) employing third parties, (vii) negotiating contracts, (viii) following procurement laws, and (ix) assuming responsibility for solid waste management from the local councils. The board is also charged with hospital, livestock, and industrial hazardous waste management, including septage and sludge retrieved from the wastewater treatment plants. It is envisaged that the board will have access to provincial budget allocations and will be in a strong position to negotiate with potential markets for recyclables, compost, refuse-derived fuel, and electricity by-products that might be generated during waste treatment.

Sector Structure and Assets Ownership

Under previous local government and health laws, all waste is owned by municipal bodies once it is placed outside premises for collection. The municipal bodies will continue to have this ownership and will be required to pay toward cost recovery for the new systems implemented by the SSWMB. As needed, equipment and facilities will be turned over to the SSWMB.

This structure implies that all local government assets and liabilities in the solid waste sector are to be turned over to the board over time, as the board becomes ready to undertake new systems and services in each jurisdiction. The board functions as a special financing vehicle to support the local governments technically and financially for the integrated management of solid waste in the province.

Sector Performance and Main Issues

Municipal solid waste management service is underperforming in Karachi. Only 40 percent of the estimated current municipal solid waste of 12,000 tons per day is transported to open dumpsites, less than 20 percent of the medical waste is well incinerated, and all the manure from two cattle farms with about 350,000 head is flushed into a drain that discharges directly into the sea. The concentrated health and environmental impacts of inadequate solid waste management practices in a city the size of Karachi constitute a severe public health hazard. The effects of carcinogenic dioxins, furans, and volatilized heavy metals and refractory organics that are discharged throughout the city are covered in appendix G. The six main issues to be addressed in developing management solutions for the solid waste sector in Karachi are as follows:

Expertise: technical expertise for immediate and long-term sector planning and phased development, as well as for finance planning and development of a fiscal impact minimization strategy.

Legal and financial instruments: appropriate legal instruments to support the design of a viable solid waste management system that addresses full collection, transport and safe disposal, institutional fragmentation among stakeholders, and a plan for cost-recovery issues.

Technical feasibility: site investigations and feasibility, geotechnical, and topographic studies that could provide data for bidding documents for private sector participation in the development of transfer stations, sanitary landfill, concession contracts, and so forth.

Markets: market studies to inform the design of an optimal system to reduce the amount of subsidy needed for operations and maintenance as well as pricing requirements for recycling and resource recovery facilities.

Cost recovery: "willingness and ability to pay" studies to inform cost recovery needed from households, businesses, cantonment boards, and establishments, as well as studies for environmental and social safeguards.

Access to finance: access to reliable and predictable finance to realize the technical assistance for immediate and long-term sector planning and phased development and investment needs.

Sector Reform and Institutional Development Needs

The solid waste sector policy has been reformed. However, regulations are needed to accompany the new solid waste and environmental acts, supported with capacity building. This applies to both the SSWMB and Environmental Protection Agency. The board needs a set of comprehensive binding agreements with each of its local government members, cantonments, and key waste generator groups.

Investment Needs and Financing

Based on current tonnage and transportation to dumpsites, the solid waste sector will need capital investment of about US$131 million per year over the next six years, totaling about US$800 million. This is based on the following assumptions: current tonnage of 12,000 per day, with 40 percent transported to dumpsites. Capital would be paid annually through long-term, private-sector contracts. The cost-recovery need is roughly US$17 per capita per year, and there is a need to explore sources of cost recovery.

Full service for the collection and transport of all waste could entail a threefold increase in the current expenditure of about US$60 million in Karachi over the lifetime of the landfill. An additional 50 percent of this will likely be needed to enable full, safe disposal (leading to a total cost of US$70 per ton), if planned and implemented carefully.

The board's budget for clearing backlogged uncollected wastes, for front-end collection of wastes, and for six waste transfer stations is US$58.23 million (about PRs 6 billion).[13] Projects for transfer stations amounting to US$27.83 million have been approved, and procurement is advanced.

Near-term investments are needed to focus on new transfer stations and new sanitary landfills. Actions will include (i) closure of existing official dumpsites and (ii) development of private-sector concession design-build-operate (DBO) arrangements for potential treatment demonstration projects: hospital waste treatment, refuse-derived fuel generation for the cement industry, and anaerobic digestion of cattle farm manure.

There may be a need to optimize contracts to better leverage the private sector to manage performance and risks. For example, GoS may wish to consider switching to a 20-year PBC for transfer stations, and creating a standardized tender. This would enable shared risks with the private sector for design, investment, and implementation, while GoS would be able to focus on supervision and monitoring of performance measures.

The board should explore which SWM services can be partially covered by user charges, gate fees, and taxes. Studies should be undertaken on whether some private (door-to-door waste, hospital waste, cattle manure, and construction or demolition waste) collection, treatment, and disposal can be covered by user charges and gate fees. Municipal services taxes could cover a portion of city cleaning and waste management.

Recommendations

1. Reforms have been initiated, with the formation of the new SSWMB, but details have yet to be developed. Further activities are needed to smooth the transition of regional planning and improvements to the systems of waste transfer, disposal, and treatment, taking into consideration how best to optimize some aspects of local involvement and governance. These include the following:
   i. Review existing laws in light of the new act and create a contract of agreement between each local government and the board. The agreements must be carefully crafted to specify roles, responsibilities, funding, and authorities.

ii. Reforms are needed to upgrade cost recovery and develop markets for waste by-products. These include user fees, gate fees, pricing policies for renewable energy and compost, and preferential procurement incentives for recyclables and recovered resources.

iii. Reforms are needed relating to transitioning some systems to licensed private service providers instead of government-paid contractors. This transition is possible for those types of wastes considered to have a viable private market or potential of private-sector participation, such as hazardous and infectious medical wastes, cattle feedlot manure, construction/demolition debris, and industrial wastes from large generators.

iv. Operations, coordination/cooperation, and monitoring will require regional and local governance capacity building. Capacity is also needed to plan, design, and procure the planned facility investments in the transfer and safe disposal or treatment of wastes.

Short-Term Next Steps for GoS

1. The SSWMB follow-up steps include the following:
    i. Conduct consultations and develop legal agreements between key stakeholder parties and the SSWMB.
    ii. Build a program of support that focuses on transfer stations and sanitary landfills, including closure of the official dump sites.
    iii. Transfer land ownership to the board for the four larger transfer station sites and the three landfill sites.
    iv. Conduct site investigations demonstrating the transfer station sites' geotechnical and topographic conditions to enable bidders to have adequate data.
    v. Prepare preliminary environmental impact assessments (EIAs) for the transfer station sites.
    vi. Develop design-build-operate-transfer tender documents to incorporate the surveys and EIA information, including any required mitigation measures that are identified.
    vii. Conduct social inclusion studies of the approximately 60,000 informal sector people involved in waste recycling, including the approximately 10,000 people living on the city dump sites.
    viii. Conduct feasibility studies for the sanitary landfills to develop conceptual designs and costs.
    ix. Conduct preliminary EIAs for the landfill sites.
    x. Study the environmental monitoring capacity needed to support the long-term solid waste system and outline the field and laboratory requirements and costs.

Long-Term Next Steps

1. Develop procurement strategy and detailed technical studies:
    i. Conduct DBO concession contract procurements for the transfer stations.

ii. Conduct detailed designs for the sanitary landfills, including mitigation measures to address the preliminary EIAs and closure activities for wastes dumped onto a small portion of two of the sites (less than 20 percent of the site areas).

iii. Develop tender documents for DBO concession contracts for the sanitary landfills.

iv. Conduct feasibility study of rail transport of wastes to the eastern sanitary landfill.

v. Determine location of rail sidings for loading and unloading, if viable.

vi. Obtain land for rail transport, if viable.

vii. Develop tender documents for DBO concession contracts of rail transport, if viable.

viii. Conduct market studies and pricing requirements for recycling and resource-recovery facilities to be located at the sanitary landfills, on a modest scale for demonstration purposes but large enough to be economically viable. Determine the spatial needs for the long term if these demonstrations were to prove successful.

ix. Develop DBO concession contract tender documents for the recycling and resource-recovery facilities, sized as demonstrations, to confirm market demand and revenue viability.

x. Repeat the steps of feasibility study and DBO concession (possibly, PPP versus an outsourced private sector participation contract) tender document development for treatment of hospital waste and cattle farm manure.

Notes

1. Population of Karachi Division (six districts), per the Pakistan Population Census 2017, Pakistan Bureau of Statistics. Various unofficial sources estimate the city's population to be higher.

2. These are generally areas observed from satellite imagery that have some ongoing development, with trunk infrastructure such as a road grid, but with adjacent land parcels that appear vacant or only partially built.

3. Based on satellite imagery, an extensive road network has been in place in the Clifton area since 2001, although much of the land has not been developed.

4. These are areas that are detected as green areas in an urban setting. It does not necessarily mean that they are accessible to the public or are public spaces such as parks.

5. Karachi Strategic Development Plan 2020.

6. *Chingchi*s are motorcycle-powered rickshaws that can fit as many as nine persons.

7. JICA 2010–11 Karachi Household Survey as part of the Karachi Transport Master Plan.

8. Sajjad et al. (2017) present substantial evidence on women's use of public transport relative to men and preferences of men and women regarding the use of various current and proposed public transport interventions for women. The study is based in Lahore, Pakistan's second-largest city after Karachi and the capital of Punjab province.

9. Karachi Electric is the privately owned company with the mandate of electricity distribution in Karachi.

10. High-rise buildings that have multiple units but are one connection are counted as a single connection. KWSB is the bulk supplier to about 18 large establishments, including defense institutions, Karachi Port Trust, Pakistan Railways, Pakistan Steel, Cantonment Boards, and public and private housing schemes.

11. The board was established through an act in 2014 that outlines the overarching goals of the board but leaves room for plans and programs to be decided later. This offers a platform for future technical assistance in developing strategies, key indicators, performance measures, and programs in addition to rules and regulations.

12. Members include the Environmental Protection Agency, KMC, DMCs, District Councils, chamber of commerce, cantonment boards, and Defence Housing Authority.

13. Per the SSWMB Annual Development Program FY2015–16.

References

ADB (Asian Development Bank). 2005. *Karachi Mega Cities Preparation Project: Final Report*, vol. 1. Manila: ADB.

Amirtahmasebi, R., and S. Kim. 2014. *Beyond Economic Growth: Livability Performance in SAR Cities*. Background paper, World Bank, Washington, DC.

Hasan, Arif. 2013. "Value Extraction from Land and Real Estate in Karachi," in *Global Gentrifications: Uneven Development and Displacement*, ed. Loretta Lees, Hyun Bang Shin, and Ernesto Lopez-Morales. Chicago: University of Chicago Press.

Hasan, Arif, Noman Ahmed, Mansoor Raza, Asiya Sadiq-Polack, Saeed Uddin Ahmed, and Moizza B. Sarwar. 2015. *Karachi: The Land Issue*. Oxford: Oxford University Press.

JICA (Japan International Cooperation Agency). 2007. *Water Supply and Sanitation Master Plan for Karachi*. Tokyo: JICA. http://open_jicareport.jica.go.jp/pdf /11888070_02.pdf.

————. 2011. *Karachi Household Survey 2010–2011*. Tokyo: JICA.

Mercer. 2014. "Quality of Living Survey." New York: Mercer. https://www.mercer.com/ne wsroom/2014-quality-of-living-survey.html.

Sajjad, Fizzah, Ghulam Abbas Anjum, Erica Field, and Kate Vyborny. 2017. *Gender Equity in Transport Planning: Improving Women's Access to Public Transport in Pakistan*. Policy brief by Consortium for Development Policy Research (CDPR).

United Nations Statistical Division. 2014. *Population and Vital Statistics Report*. New York: UN.

World Wildlife Fund for Nature. 2007. *Pakistan's Waters at Risk: Water and Health-Related Issues in Pakistan and Key Recommendations*. WWF–Pakistan, https://reliefweb.int /sites/reliefweb.int/files/resources/B6BEACFD60CE8E4AC125777D00478896 -Full_Report.pdf.

CHAPTER 4

Pathway 3: City Sustainability and Inclusiveness

Fiscal Risks to Sustainability

Inadequate availability of financing is a key constraint on reducing the infrastructure and service-delivery gaps in Karachi. This is true at both the provincial and local government levels. The previous chapter estimated that Karachi needs between US$9 billion and US$10 billion in financing over a two-year period to meet its infrastructure and service-delivery needs in three sectors: (i) urban transport, (ii) water supply and sanitation, and (iii) municipal solid waste (see table 4.1). This section discusses constraints and fiscal risks at the provincial and local government levels that hinder the city's progress in mobilizing and spending financial resources to meet these needs.

Current infrastructure spending in Karachi by the public sector is well below these requirements, despite recent large increases. The provincial government is spending at least US$110 million per year in Karachi for rehabilitation of infrastructure.[1] The local governments are heavily constrained and are able to spend only about one-tenth of their budget—around US$14 million per year, in the case of the Karachi Metropolitan Corporation (KMC)—for capital expenditure. The availability of public financing for Karachi's needs is limited, which substantially increases its opportunity cost.

At the Provincial Level

Collections of the urban immovable property tax (UIPT) from Karachi (and Sindh) remain dismal compared with the potential. Global experience shows that the urban property tax is an important source of financing to meet the infrastructure and service-delivery needs of cities. In Sindh, as in other provinces of Pakistan, the UIPT is collected by the provincial government and then partly transferred to various local entities and municipal service providers (after deduction of a collection fee). The government of Sindh (GoS) and its departments have authority over determining the tax base, rate schedule, exemptions,

Table 4.1 Karachi's Estimated Infrastructure Needs and Costs over 10 Years

Sector	Estimated cost over 10 years (US$)
Urban transport	5.5 billion–6.0 billion
Water supply and sanitation	2.5 billion–3.0 billion
Municipal solid waste	1.0 billion
Total	9.0 billion–10.0 billion

collection mechanisms, and all other facets of this tax. Given the size of Karachi's economy and real estate base, the city contributes a lion's share to Sindh's total UIPT revenue.

However, revenue from urban property tax in Sindh is extremely low compared with the potential. Punjab province collects four times as much in UIPT as Sindh every year (figure 4.1). In comparison, Indian cities are far ahead; a single Indian metropolitan city collects many times more in annual property taxes than Sindh. Sindh's UIPT collections as a share of urban gross domestic product (GDP) are only a quarter of the average for middle-income countries (figure 4.2). Increasing revenue from the UIPT is essential to finance infrastructure needs in Karachi.

At the Local Government, Municipal Level

Local governments in Karachi have a very small fiscal and financial management capacity. They have limited authority over major sources of revenue, such as urban property taxes. Policies and practices across all aspects of fiscal and financial management in local governments are considered basic to lacking. This weak capacity is a result of several factors:

1. Volatile institutional framework for local governments and intraprovincial governmental relations, marked by frequent changes and high unpredictability
2. Division and fragmentation of mandates for urban development and service delivery across multiple entities
3. Very low, nascent, or deteriorating capacity and systems at local governments in the city (and province)

Karachi city governments are financially weak, with a high dependence on fiscal transfers from GoS. Those transfers—in the shape of mandated regular transfers (defined by the previously constituted Provincial Finance Commission award) and matching grants in lieu of the now-repealed Octroi and Zila Tax—account for as much as 75 percent of annual operating revenue for the KMC and 87 percent for one District Municipal Corporation (DMC) in the city. These transfers can be unpredictable and are often delayed. This leads to cities having difficulty managing their revenue and expenditure flows. Revenues are mostly collected centrally by the federal government and are distributed between the federal and provincial governments based on the National Finance Commission

Figure 4.1 Urban Property Tax Collection in Sindh Is Much Lower Than in Punjab (Pakistan) and Selected Indian Cities

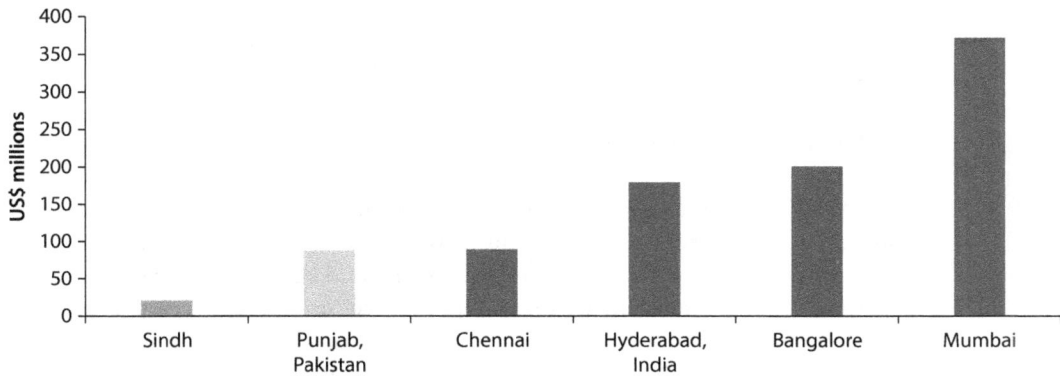

Source: World Bank analysis based on official budget data for FY2015–16.

Figure 4.2 Urban Property Tax–to–Urban GDP Ratio in Sindh Is Very Low Compared to Punjab, Selected Indian Cities, and Middle-Income Country Average

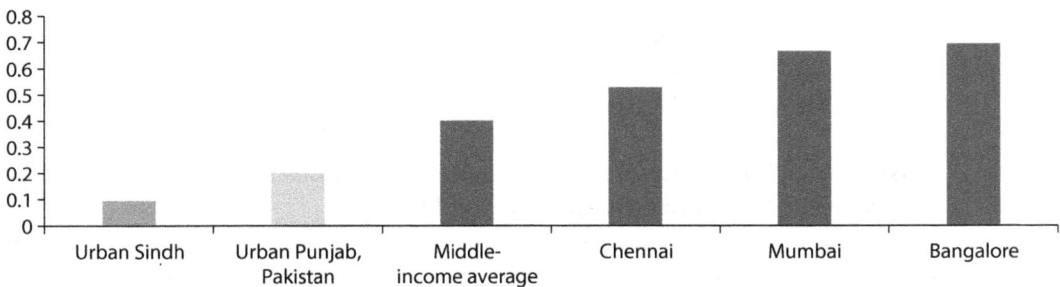

Sources: World Bank analysis, based on official budget data for FY2015–16. Middle-income average from Norregaard 2013. Urban GDP estimates from World Bank 2014 and McKinsey 2011.
Note: GDP = gross domestic product.

Award. Provinces raise their own resources via sales taxes on services, excise duties, property taxes, and so forth. Transfers to municipalities are then determined by each provincial government separately.

Very Low Collections of Own-Source Revenues

The small size of local government revenues is grossly insufficient to cover essential services and infrastructure needs. Collections from self-collected or own-source revenues (OSR) are very low compared with the potential, due to poor enforcement. KMC audit reports by the auditor general of Pakistan (AGP) estimate that city governments fail to collect up to 90 percent of potential OSR. The KMC's own estimates indicate that it currently recovers only 7 percent of the potential of one source: municipal utility charges and taxes. The poor enforcement effort also leads to a gap between the budgeted and actual revenues. During FYs 2014–17, the KMC collected only around 30 percent of what it budgeted as revenue. Weak revenue management has substantial negative spillovers to other aspects of financial management, such as expenditure and liquidity management. Municipalities are also constrained in their ability to raise OSRs by the requirement to seek approval from GoS for increases in certain tax and fee rates.

High Inflexibility in Expenditure and Weak Expenditure-Management Practices

An overwhelming share of the expenditure of the KMC and other municipalities is in recurrent and operating expenses and the day-to-day running of government. During FYs 2014–17, recurrent and operating expenditure has accounted for 90 percent of total expenditure, on average, leaving only 10 percent for capital expenditure such as infrastructure development. Salaries and other employee-related costs have accounted for an average of 70 percent of operating expenditure, reflecting a very large payroll. It is also believed that there are large number of "ghost" employees—unfilled positions created irregularly to collect salaries. AGP audit reports of the KMC also point out other irregularities, such as withdrawals from bank accounts of large sums without accompanying supporting documentation, awarding of large works without following the tender process, and other anomalies. These issues remain unaddressed and point to severe weaknesses in the city's expenditure-management processes.

Issues with Transparency and the Disclosure of Financial Statements, Exacerbated by an Insufficient Auditing Process

Although annual financial statements are prepared by municipalities, they are done so in a rudimentary way. The annual budgets are essentially a simplistic listing of revenue and expenditure for each line item in the budget. Audits by the AGP are confined to a narrow scope—transactions relating to procurement and procedures. There is no certification of accounts or an opinion on the reliability of the statements. But even in this narrow scope of audit, serious findings have been flagged in the past few years and require substantial improvements. Because of the limited prosecution powers of AGP and no action taken by the provincial Public Accounts Committee, the same audit findings are repeated in the AGP's audit reports every year.

Low and Unpredictable Revenue Leads to Weak and Unreliable Budgeting

The lack of a substantial OSR base means that municipalities must rely solely on fiscal transfers from GoS to meet expenses. While these transfers do come monthly, as stipulated, they are often late. This has an impact on budgeting and expenditure planning. Revenues coming in significantly below budget means that the KMC usually must revise its budget in the middle of the fiscal year, with the magnitude of the revisions made being very large—close to 30 percent downward revision of expenditure during FYs 2014–17, on average.

Low Reserves and Weak Liquidity Management Also Pose High Fiscal Risk
The KMC's cash balances are very low, and it has limited access to cash lines from banks. Its end-of-month cash balances over the period from January to June 2016 were enough to cover only 3 percent of monthly operating expenditure on average, that is, only one day of operating expenditure. Not only are payments to suppliers often materially late, salaries are almost always paid late too, depending on when fiscal transfers from the provincial government are made. The situation would be the same in DMCs in Karachi.

Compared to peer cities in other developing countries, Karachi is considered very weak in financial management. Peer cities in Indonesia and the Philippines have better processes and systems. It is also worth noting that they operate in a public finance environment that has stronger institutions with much better political stability. This sets a more benign stage for them compared to Karachi.

Recommendations
1. Increase revenue from urban property taxes to invest in Karachi. GoS should invest in updating and modernizing the entire UIPT system and increase enforcement to raise revenue. The following specific actions are proposed:
   i. Invest in the modernization and automation of the property tax system.
   ii. Conduct a comprehensive survey of properties and rate areas in cities, beginning with Karachi, to identify the full tax net; digitize the entire property tax record and create computerized billing and collection systems. Punjab has already made substantial progress in this effort in six of its largest cities, and this approach can be replicated in Sindh.
   iii. Increase tax net coverage by using all built-up urban areas as rating areas.
   iv. Update valuation tables to reflect market values of land and establish a schedule to update them more regularly. See box 4.1 for a relevant example from Colombia.
   v. Reduce the differential between owner-occupied and rental property, which distorts the rental housing market by creating a disincentive to use housing units for rent.
   vi. Introduce property taxes on developed vacant land to discourage speculative plot holdings, release land for productive uses, and enhance revenue.
2. Improve fiscal resources available to local governments to fulfill their mandates. GoS should revise and update the fiscal transfer mechanism—the Provincial Financial Commission (PFC) Award—for local governments based on international best practices. The following specific actions are proposed:
   i. Revise the PFC Award formula, ensuring that allocations for all local governments (urban and rural) and associated agencies and entities are based on needs, functions, and size, along with criteria for backwardness, poverty, and performance.

Box 4.1 Updating the Cadaster to Increase Property Tax Revenue: The Case of Colombia

In the mid-2000s, Bogotá, the capital city of Colombia, was experiencing a real estate boom, but the local government was forgoing important revenues because of an outdated property tax base. To capture those gains and raise finances for a new subway line, the mayor of Bogotá initiated a major update of physical records and taxation values for 2.1 million properties.

The reassessment work included three major components: the *physical* revision of parcels' configuration, *legal* updates that verified ownership, and *economic* changes to assessment values, using research from the real estate market. The improvements cost less than US$15 million, or about $6.50 per parcel.

Because of the program, the cadastral value increased 47 percent, from US$66.5 billion in 2008 to US$98 billion in 2010. Property tax revenues increased by US$171 million, and reached 40 percent of own-source revenues for the local government.

To avoid a shock from dramatically increased property tax bills, Bogotá's city council implemented a ceiling that increased the tax over time. This approach had two main benefits. First, it shielded the technical updating of the cadaster from the political implications of raising taxes; and second, it smoothed tax increases for property owners, reducing uncertainty and lessening resistance.

Among the factors leading to the success of these efforts were strong political support, the technical capacity of cadastral agencies to revalue properties, and a clear policy to avoid sudden increases in tax bills.

Source: Adapted from Farvacque-Vitkovic and Kopanyi 2014.

---

      ii. Create a mechanism for performance-based grants to local governments, to regulate transfers outside the PFC Award, using best practices available in developing countries.

     iii. Ensure predictable, scheduled, and automatic fiscal transfers from the province to all local governments, on the pattern of the National Finance Commission Award transfers from the federal level to provinces.

3. Improve financial management in local governments and related entities. GoS should work closely with local governments to eliminate the substantial gaps in financial management at the local level and improve the efficiency of public expenditure. The following specific actions are proposed:

     i. Improve budgetary practices. The annual budget anchors many aspects of financial management. Improving budget forecasting and development and synchronizing the budget to a medium-term framework, along with better execution, will lead to positive spillovers to various aspects of financial management. Budgets developed by local governments are often unrealistic, based on high estimates of revenue that do not materialize during the year, resulting in mid-year downward revisions. In addition, development budgets are not aligned with longer-term development strategies.

ii. Enhance OSR collections for local governments to gradually reduce their reliance on provincial fiscal transfers. This involves conducting comprehensive surveys to assess the full potential of and tax base for revenue sources, modern methods of billing and collection, communication campaigns, rationalization for rates and bases for each local tax and fee, and an assessment of the political economy of each local tax and fee.

iii. Improve transparency, disclosure, and auditing practices. This entails producing detailed financial statements for local governments—including balance sheets, cash-flow statements, reconciliation statements, and so forth—which will improve transparency and disclosure. For this to take place, as a first step the AGP and relevant GoS departments (such as the finance and local government departments) will be required to revise the formats in which local governments prepare budgets and accounts statements, to align them with modern best practices. Further, all local governments must be made to take steps to address pending audit recommendations and observations identified in annual audits by AGP.

Environmental Sustainability and Climate-Change Risks

Environment

Karachi is confronted with severe environmental challenges that affect productivity and economic growth. Due a high incidence of air, land, and water (including marine) pollution that results from inadequate management of solid and hazardous waste—including medical waste, raw sewage, industrial effluent, and vehicular pollution—a large proportion of Karachi residents are prone to diseases linked to environmental pollution. A World Bank (2015) study estimated that the annual cost of environmental health impacts in Sindh is about PRs 371 billion, which is equal to 10 percent of provincial GDP. It is assumed that 70 percent (PRs 260 billion) of this cost occurs in Karachi.

Health costs related to air pollution in Karachi are estimated in the range of PRs 30 billion–40 billion every year. The presence of high concentrations of pollutants in the air of Karachi causes multiple types of respiratory diseases among its residents. Twenty-three percent of the patients admitted to the Civil Hospital were diagnosed with respiratory tract infections (IUCN 2007).

Open burning of industrial solid waste and the discharge of untreated liquid waste are serious hazards in Karachi. Recent fatalities occurred due to direct exposure of people to the burning of industrial toxic solid waste. In the absence of effluent treatment plants, industrial liquid waste containing oil, heavy metals, and toxic chemicals is discharged directly into the rivers and has affected human and marine life considerably. Drinking water appears to be a major source of lead exposure. A World Bank study looking at 18 towns of Karachi city revealed blood lead concentration exceeding the WHO guideline in 89 percent of the sampled sources (World Bank 2010). Elevated blood lead levels are known to result in learning disabilities in children and reduced income later in life.

Recommendations

1. "Green" the public infrastructure. Many interventions to address environmental pollution are integral to infrastructure sectors such as transport and waste management. For example, the opportunity presented by a bus rapid transit project could be used to push for low-emission buses, remove old polluting buses, create signal-free corridors, construct better roads, and so forth to facilitate a modal shift from private cars to public transport. This would reduce congestion and improve air quality.
2. Provide environmental infrastructure. Certain types of infrastructure—such as common effluent treatment plants for liquid industrial waste, wastewater treatment works for domestic effluents, associated laboratory facilities for quality control, and air-quality monitoring stations for ambient air, among other efforts—fall under the category of environmental infrastructure. These are required to address some of the key environmental issues and challenges.
3. Strengthen environmental regulations and institutions. Make the role of the Environmental Protection Agency more effective by putting in place a better and up-to-date regulatory framework, complemented with an efficient institutional setup that has qualified and capable personnel. This would be critical in providing a framework for and guidance on how to efficiently manage and maintain the infrastructure, and will result in a more effective command-and-control plan to address environmental pollution.

Disaster Risks and Climate Resilience

Karachi is one of the most vulnerable cities of Pakistan, prone to different kinds of hazards and threats—natural as well as human-made—due to its unique geoclimatic conditions. It is at high risk of disasters, such as floods, earthquakes, tsunamis, cyclones, water scarcity, heat waves, and fire. According to the federal government's National Disaster Management Plan 2012–22, Karachi is ranked as the most vulnerable to disaster of all districts of Pakistan.

Policy and Institutional Framework

The National Disaster Management Act of 2010 established a three-tiered disaster-management system, at federal, provincial, and district levels. The Provincial Disaster Management Authority Sindh was established as the implementing agency at the provincial level. Similarly, District Disaster Management Authorities (DDMAs) were constituted for the district governments in Karachi. However, the DDMAs have weak integration, rudimentary structures, and limited planning and operational capacity to respond to disaster events.

Sector Performance and Main Issues

Several underlying issues affect the government's performance in this area.

Emergency planning and disaster management services are not sufficient. The roles and responsibilities of city authorities in disaster-management services are not well understood or executed, current structures are inappropriate, and resource allocation is insufficient. Critically, concerned agencies experience gaps in information on vulnerability, and there is a lack of integrated planning and coordinated response among key actors, such as provincial authorities and DDMAs, rescue and emergency health care services, and firefighting.

Weak land-planning, building-control, and enforcement functions directly affect performance in terms of emergency access to settlements, resilience of the built-up area, and planning for emergency health care facilities. Safety standards have not been stringently enforced, and there is a serious disconnect between building bylaws and existing capacity of such agencies as the Karachi fire department. Fire alarm systems, smoke detectors, sprinklers, fire extinguishers, fire escapes, and emergency exits are missing from most buildings.

Municipal service delivery in areas such as water supply, sanitation, solid waste management, and urban environment is linked to disaster management. In particular, mitigating flood risks is intrinsically linked to the expansion and improvement of urban drainage infrastructure. The inadequate storm water drains currently operating are clogged due to the dumping of solid waste, are encroached upon, and invariably carry sewage and effluent, which inhibits their capacity to discharge storm water from areas prone to flooding.

Structural preparedness against seismic shocks, urban flooding, and other events is inadequate. The poor structural preparedness of existing buildings is a result of deficient building codes that are not supported by adequate risk information, weak enforcement, poor capacity in the private construction sector, and low awareness among local residents. According to a recent seismic vulnerability assessment of Karachi supported by the World Bank, a very high number of existing structures would incur moderate to complete damage in the event of a high-intensity earthquake in Karachi, and many areas and communities are at high risk from urban flooding. Vulnerable structures also include a significant number of public buildings, hospitals, and schools, among others (NED University, n.d.).

Recommendations

1. Conduct a vulnerability assessment of critical and essential facilities. The objective is to develop the consensus-driven analytical foundation required for longer-term investments to reduce risk in the built environment of Karachi. Building on the multihazard risk assessment of Karachi, a first activity would concentrate on a census survey of the vulnerability of the built environment in Karachi to earthquakes and hydrometeorological events, focusing on essential and critical facilities and infrastructure, such as road links, bridges, health facilities, schools, and public offices. The second activity is the development of risk-sensitive land-use planning.

Transforming Karachi into a Livable and Competitive Megacity
http://dx.doi.org/10.1596/978-1-4648-1211-8

2. Reinforce Karachi's emergency-management response capacity. An emergency-management system needs to be put in place that will mobilize resources at all levels and assign roles and responsibilities more efficiently. Activities would include the following:
   i.   Develop integrated, citywide emergency-management plans.
   ii. Renovate and outfit city-level Disaster Risk Management (DRM) facilities.
   iii. Build, renovate, and outfit local-level DDMA, fire service, and emergency response facilities in Karachi.
   iv. Supply, install, and integrate specialized emergency management and communications technology equipment for DRM and emergency response in local-level agencies.
   v.   Supply specialized search-and-rescue equipment to local-level agencies involved in DRM for scaling up existing interventions, such as Rescue 1299.
   vi. Provide training, exercises, and drills to local-level agencies involved in DRM.

3. Improve construction, urban planning, and development. The objective of this intervention would be to put in place the institutional infrastructure and competency needed to reduce long-term disaster vulnerability in Karachi. It would address both the existing and future built environment. The overall scheme would cover four areas of investment: (i) create a unit within the provincial government and the KMC to support the integration of risk information into development planning; (ii) establish the infrastructure and processes at the KMC and the Sindh Building Control Authority (SBCA) to ensure an efficient and integrated mechanism for land-use and zoning clearance, permitting, and approval of site and building plans; (iii) improve competency through professional accreditation, training, continuous education, and forums; and (iv) strengthen building-code implementation and enforcement. The following activities may be implemented:
   i.   Create and operationalize urban resilience units at GoS's Planning and Development Department as well as at the KMC.
   ii. Establish an electronic construction permitting system at the KMC and SBCA.
   iii. Set up a professional accreditation program for engineers, architects, and planners.
   iv. Improve building-code enforcement under SBCA.

Social Risks to Sustainability

Karachi is a city of migrants with various ethnic diversities, which impacts its social fabric. The ethnic diversity resulting from different waves of migration did not develop into full-blown cosmopolitanism but instead created pockets of ethnically homogenous zones within an extremely heterogeneous city.

Although Karachi does not appear on the United Nations' top-50 ranking of violent cities as gauged by the murder rate, violence remains a feature of daily life for most of the city's residents, especially the poorest. Indeed, the normalization of violence has created a vision of the city where Karachiites cannot imagine a future without it (Gayer 2014). Yet, the experience of other cities demonstrates that evidence-based, targeted urban policies can significantly reduce violence and promote a more inclusive city.

Urban Segregation

Exclusionary urban planning. Since the colonial era, and through partition to the present day, Karachi has dealt with a constant tension between formal and informal structures (Gazdar 2011). Karachi is a city of migrants, with insufficient urban planning to absorb the exponential flow of people into anything near an adequate formal structure of housing and other services. Within migrant groups, partition migrants are perceived to have been favored above other cohorts that existed before or arrived later. Urban planning initiatives in Karachi have been inadequate in providing formal housing for most residents, and in some cases have exacerbated the problem by displacing residents to build physical infrastructure (Banerjee, Chaudhury, and Das 2005).

Housing and land contestations. Only one-third of the 75,500 new housing units required in Karachi each year are provided by the formal private and public sectors. As a result, land agents have emerged as key players in Karachi's urban development and have accrued great wealth and power in the process (Gayer 2014). As the demand for housing in Karachi has grown, informal land developers have become increasingly aggressive in their attempts to acquire land to be developed unofficially. These informal actors, known locally as the "land mafias" (Gayer 2014; Inskeep 2011), often operate through corrupt and violent means. Even though the informalization of formal processes has given low-income residents access to many affordable plots, these are usually far from their workplace or from the city center where better social facilities are available (Hasan et al. 2015), exacerbating the urban exclusion of populations in informal areas.

The development of informal settlements has historically been linked to the city's informal economy. For example, in the 1980s, Karachi became a main hub of the overland heroin trade. Criminal syndicates involved in this trade reinvested their illegal profits in informal land settlements and private transport networks. Garments, leather goods, and carpets are all produced in the informal settlements. Intermediaries provide training, materials, equipment, and cash for the production of these items, which takes place in people's homes, on a contract basis (Hasan 2002). As a result, exporters and industrialists can reduce production costs and prevent the unionization of labor and the application of labor laws and the minimum wage (Hasan 2002), creating a political economy that has no incentives to address informality.

Informality of service delivery. The proliferation of informal settlements has also led to the growth of informal service-delivery channels. Forty-five percent of the electricity consumed in the city comes through illegal connections to the Karachi Electric Supply Company's network, provided by land agents or unofficial electricity suppliers to the city's vast informal settlements (Gayer 2014). More than

42 percent of the water supply moves through an informal network of privately owned water tankers,[2] and up to one-third of the city's solid waste is separated and recycled through informal processes. The informal sector also provides most of the transport infrastructure used by Karachi's residents. Official service delivery is fragmented between provincial and local governments. To date, the regularization of informal settlements has often been ad hoc, partial, and politicized (Hasan et al. 2015). Widespread informality necessitates interlocutors to fill the major gaps in formal service delivery: these can be land agents, criminal syndicates, or local-level affiliates of political parties.

Social Exclusion

Proliferation of informal settlements and slums. Karachi's unplanned areas can be divided into three main subcategories: (i) *katchi abadis* that have been regularized or are awaiting regularization; (ii) slums, which are very dense inner city areas with deficient infrastructure; and (iii) villages, or goths, which have become part of the urban sprawl. Often, these different types of unplanned areas are mixed together and recognized as *katchi abadis*. According to estimates, over 50 percent of Karachiites live in informal settlements of various types.

Urban poverty has become a concern in Karachi. In *katchi abadis*, most of the inhabitants lack sufficient income, permanent jobs, tenure security, and access to services and infrastructure (Hasan et al. 2015). Furthermore, poor living conditions and unhygienic environments have exposed them to ill health and low productivity, limiting their capacity to generate income and avail proper livelihoods (Mahbub ul Haq Human Development Centre 2014). Qualitative research led by local researchers shows that residents of *katchi abadis* have often expressed a sense of self-deprivation where they are stripped of their "rights to the city" and stuck in a cyclical poverty trap (Hasan et al. 2015).

Gender risks to men and women. Similar to other violent urban centers, young men are particularly vulnerable to be recruited for violent acts in Karachi. In Pakistan, more than 67 percent of the population is under the age of 25, and Karachi has similar demography, putting young men, predominantly in less-well-off areas, at risk of recruitment into violent gangs. Some of the major reasons behind youth involvement in violence are poverty, lack of education opportunities, and "limited access to positive social interactions" (Search for Common Ground Pakistan 2014). Women in Karachi have increasingly become victims of the violence in the city. Beyond domestic violence, Karachi has witnessed the assassination of several of its female activists in recent years.

Fragmented Institutional Arrangements

Institutions tasked with overseeing urban development and institutional responses to Karachi's planning challenges have, conversely, contributed to urban segregation and social exclusion. This can mainly be attributed to the inadequacy of institutional arrangements for governance and service delivery, which have led to gaps that deepen divisions between formal and informal areas, migrant groups, and ethnic groups. This subsection highlights some of the shortcomings of Karachi's institutional structures and systems.

Elite power contestation—local versus provincial. While Karachi is the political and economic center of Sindh, it is also the center for the struggle for political representation and access by several ethnic communities. Conflict between political parties has resulted in the question of whether Karachi should be governed at the provincial or city level.[3] The existence of the Pakistan People's Party (PPP)–led provincial government and a Muttahida Qaumi Movement (MQM)–led city government has resulted in the question of whether Karachi should be governed at the provincial or city level. It has also, over time, led to violence and to the formation of informal structures. Shifts between the two systems have created governance gaps that have been filled by informal service providers and have exacerbated grievances between ethnic groups. The fear of losing influence at the local level has also led to aggressive turf wars and rent-seeking behaviors by informal actors. The proliferation of informal settlements in Karachi is exacerbated by the fact that the city's development falls to more than 20 federal and provincial government agencies.

Elite power contestation—federal. Political dynamics at the federal level can also influence the city's politics. The MQM has been an important player in the coalition politics that have defined much of Pakistan's trajectory during its democratic transitions. The party has entered alliances with all the major parties at the federal level—Pakistan People's Party and Pakistan Muslim League (N)—and its role at the federal level has alternately prevented federally mandated security operations in the city or caused them. These operations add another layer of complexity, since an impression can be created that a federal-level player that does not have a stake in the city's local dynamics in either formal or informal sectors can make top-down security policy decisions that have an unforeseen local impact.

Elite power contestation—military. The military is a key stakeholder of the city, with control of planned cantonment land that is developed and sold primarily to private real estate developers. Since September 2013, a paramilitary operation to restore law and order to the city has sparked a new wave of claims and counterclaims between the political parties and the paramilitary Rangers.

Clientelism. Urban segregation, social exclusion, and institutional fragmentation have led to conditions that can easily be exploited by the political parties and other groups for political gain, and the political parties in Karachi have historically collaborated primarily with informal land interlocutors to control constituents. City authorities, port authorities, military cantonment boards, and private-sector developers also vie for control of land in the city and control of lucrative planning projects. Private developers and land mafias working on behalf of the political parties acquire land through corruption, bribe officials to tamper with land records, and pit agencies against one other to ensure that amenity plots are converted and commercialized.[4] Moreover, formal actors vying for control of urban development projects often must turn to the informal sector to gain support for particular initiatives: this support can take the form of access to particular localities, labor provision, access to utilities such as electricity, and other services required for formal actors to successfully undertake urban development projects (Gayer 2014).

Recommendations

International experience shows that moving toward inclusive development while reducing chronic violence requires an integrated urban policy approach built on a close understanding of the social and spatial synergies, with emphasis on inclusive coalitions and the participation of all stakeholders in the urban space—citizens, the private sector, and represented authorities to support institutional transformation. Lessons learned from Colombia, Brazil, and South Africa show myriad development programs with integrated components for reducing violence. These programs have included local service delivery, education, urban planning through public spaces, youth inclusion and empowerment, strengthening of institutions, and supporting citizen participation.

Moving forward, confidence building, inclusive coalition, and institutional transformation need to be incorporated as crosscutting urban policy themes. The analysis of Karachi shows that socioeconomic and spatial inequalities, exclusions indicated at the city and subcity levels, and the fragmentation of institutions have generated violence and eroded the social capital of the city, and simultaneously hindered its formal governance. To be successful, all policies will need to focus on (i) social inclusion to help create fair conditions for all populations and neighborhoods in Karachi to access land and urban goods and services and contribute to social integration, and (ii) citizen participation to recognize the role of local communities and reinforce their sense of belonging to the city. A public policy that incorporates consultations and citizens' feedback can contribute to the transformation of power relations in Karachi.

First Steps for Research and Policy

1. Study tours for Karachi policy makers to Medellín, Bogotá, and Rio de Janeiro in peer exchanges to initiate a global policy dialogue for transforming Karachi. Such study tours will help build international networks and partnerships on targeted issues related to inclusion, participation, and the reduction of violence.
2. Workshops with representatives from cities such as Medellín, Bogotá, and Rio de Janeiro, which have successfully developed integrated urban policies to create a local commitment to issues of inclusion, participation, and the reduction of violence.
3. A joint research agenda between the World Bank and the city of Karachi covering issues of spatial dynamics, female labor force participation, and violence to further identify areas for immediate action in the city and help local authorities devise a strategic plan to move forward on issues of city transformation.

Consequent Operational and Technical Assistance

1. Citizen-engagement mechanisms. Capacity building, supporting citizen feedback mechanisms such as citizen score cards, creating an e-government platform for citizen engagement, and grievance redress mechanisms for projects have proven effective elsewhere.

2. Public space investment with enhanced citizen engagement. Such places should be multifunctional areas for social interaction, community building, and economic exchange. Adequate planning of public spaces is key in changing the built environment of urban centers. Giving special focus to the needs of women and other usually excluded and vulnerable groups living in or using these spaces will make them safer and their lives better. Making safe public spaces available to women will reduce the likelihood of harassment and violence, and help improve their participation in civic, public, and economic activities.

3. Urban, youth-targeted social programs for violence reduction. This can be done by providing safe spaces and healthy alternative activities for youth in urban areas. These can support music groups, sports teams, and other activities.

4. More inclusive employment-intensive infrastructure programs. Such programs need to focus on the unplanned and least privileged areas with of the city, with an emphasis on providing employment for local communities, specifically for young men.

5. Enhancing female labor force participation through interventions that target female low- and mid-skilled labor. Such interventions can mitigate women's constraints to entering the labor force. Such interventions include providing adequate, reliable, and safe public transport for women and providing gender-responsive infrastructure in the public and private sectors to allow for more women to be part of the labor force, such as affordable day care centers, working women's hostels, and so forth. These interventions will increase women's opportunities to access jobs, education, and civic opportunities.

6. Capacity building for land reforms, titling, and adjudication. This will help address the inequities of the informal system that too often determine where people can live.

7. Supporting inclusive decision making. It requires specific attention in all investment projects in the city. Analysis of vulnerabilities and barriers to inclusion of targeted beneficiaries, including women and youth, would be necessary in project preparation and design.

8. Improving safety and security for women in Karachi. This is paramount to increasing women's participation in civic life. Measures can include the establishment of more women-only police stations or allocation of women-specific desks in all police stations to address cases of violence against women and other issues. Currently, women constitute only 1.5 percent of the total police force in Sindh province.[5]

Notes

1. From the government of Sindh's Annual Development Program for fiscal years 2016–17 and 2017–18.
2. It is estimated that 90 percent of the water should be distributed through formal channels, but this is not reflected in Karachi (Anwar 2013).
3. The Pakistan People's Party running the Sindh government favors the Sindh Local Government Ordinance of 1979, which retains powers—including land and revenue allocation—at the provincial level, relies on appointed commissioners, and divides Karachi into five administrative districts. The Muttahida Quami Movement—mostly representing Mohajir postpartition migrants—favors the Sindh Local Government Act 2001, which devolves power from the province to the local level, empowers elected *nazims* (mayors), and unifies Karachi under one city district government, facilitating single-party control of the city.
4. An amenity plot is allocated exclusively for the purpose of amenity uses, as defined in Karachi Building and Town Planning Regulations 2002, such as government uses, health and welfare uses, education uses, assembly uses, religious uses, parks and play grounds, burial grounds, transportation right-of-way, parking, and recreational areas.
5. Data from the National Police Bureau, government of Pakistan.

References

Anwar, Farhan. 2013. "Karachi's Water Woes." *Dawn*, July 30.

Banerjee, Paula, Sabyasachi Chaudhury, and Samir Das. 2005. *Internal Displacement in South Asia*. Thousand Oaks, CA: Sage.

Farvacque-Vitkovic, Catherine, and Mihaly Kopanyi, eds. 2014. *Municipal Finances: A Handbook for Local Governments*. Washington, DC: World Bank.

Gayer, Laurent. 2014. *Karachi: Ordered Disorder and the Struggle for the City*. Oxford: Oxford University Press.

Gazdar, Haris. 2011. "Karachi Battles." *Economic and Political Weekly* 46 (38): 17–24.

Hasan, Arif, Noman Ahmed, Mansoor Raza, Asiya Sadiq-Polack, Saeed Uddin Ahmed, and Moizza B. Sarwar. 2015. *Karachi: The Land Issue*. Oxford: Oxford University Press.

Inskeep, Steve. 2011. *Instant City: Life and Death in Karachi*. New York: Penguin Press.

IUCN (International Union for Conservation of Nature and Natural Resources, Pakistan). 2007. "Sindh Strategy for Sustainable Development." Islamabad: IUCN Pakistan, Sindh Programme. http://cmsdata.iucn.org/downloads/sssd.pdf.

Mahbub ul Haq Human Development Centre. 2014. "The Rise of Karachi as a Mega-City: Issues and Challenges." Policy Brief. Islamabad.

McKinsey Global Institute. 2011. "Urban World: Mapping the Economic Power of Cities." New York: McKinsey & Company. https://www.mckinsey.com/~/media/McKinsey/Global%20Themes/Urbanization/Urban%20world/MGI_urban_world_mapping_economic_power_of_cities_full_report.ashx.

NED University of Engineering and Technology. N.d. *Development of Probabilistic Flood and Seismic Risk Assessment of Karachi: Technical Report*. Unpublished report.

Norregaard, John. 2013. "Taxing Immovable Property: Revenue Potential and Implementation Challenges." IMF Working Paper 13/129. Washington, DC.

Search for Common Ground Pakistan. 2014. *Progress Report 2013–2014*. Brussels: Search for Common Ground Pakistan. https://www.sfcg.org/wp-content/uploads/2014/06/Search-For-Common-Ground-Pakistan-Progress-Report-2013-2014.pdf

World Bank. 2010. *Water and Sewerage Services in Karachi: Citizen Report Card—Sustainable Service Delivery Improvements*. Washington, DC: World Bank.

———. 2014. "Pakistan Urban Sector Assessment." Background paper for South Asia Urbanization Flagship. Washington, DC: World Bank.

———. 2015. *Sustainability and Poverty Alleviation: Confronting Environmental Threats in Sindh, Pakistan*. Directions in Development. Washington, DC: World Bank.

CHAPTER 5

The Way Forward

City Priorities and Key Considerations

Karachi finds itself at a crossroads; one route may lead toward being the beacon of urbanization's promises, and the other toward being an example of its multi-faceted challenges. With increasing global competition, the largest megacity of Pakistan must act resolutely and rapidly to preserve its position as the country's main growth center and window to the world. The Karachi Metropolitan Region has a complex political environment, ad-hoc planning, poor governance, and weak financial and institutional capacities. These create significant challenges to urban infrastructure and service delivery, place constraints on competitiveness, and adversely affect the city's livability and resilience.

Four strategic pillars can be the foundation for improving Karachi City's livability and sustainability.

Pillar 1: Building inclusive, coordinated, and accountable institutions. Reforming institutions to improve the operational performance of utilities and other service providers will be necessary to prevent serious inefficiencies, such as ad-hoc urban and investment planning; revenues losses; and physical losses. With the new elected mayoral system in place, there is also an opportunity to empower the local government to take the lead in city management. This process will be made more inclusive and representative by ensuring that women and usually excluded and vulnerable groups are well represented in these institutions so that investments in infrastructure and service delivery respond to their needs.

Pillar 2: Greening Karachi for sustainability and resilience. There is a critical need to close infrastructure gaps and to safeguard maintenance spending. A focus on good maintenance offers one of the highest returns to infrastructure spending and could act as a kind of investment in asset preservation. In addition, Karachi needs to put in place buffers for vulnerable groups, including women and youth, from the negative impacts of growth and climate change while designing and implementing appropriate development programs. Finally, Karachi needs to build a resilient and sustainable environment that is focused not only on providing a good standard of municipal services but also on improving urban livability.

Enhancing and ensuring the safety of public assets such as beaches, parks, and heritage buildings are opportunities for city regeneration and transformation.

Pillar 3: Leveraging the city's economic, social, and environmental assets. Karachi cannot rely solely on public investments to close its huge infrastructure gaps. Investment needs for municipal infrastructure, including public transport, are so large that the current financing mechanisms are inadequate. Involving the private sector in infrastructure provision can have many benefits, including stronger incentives for more efficient performance and more access to capital (technical, financial, and managerial), as well as newer technologies. Potential public-private partnership projects are already preidentified in the transport, sanitation, and solid waste sectors. There are also various opportunities to better leverage the potential of what Karachi has to offer in terms of its strong economic base and physical assets—such as land, waterfronts and ports, human capital, and environmental assets—to generate better economic and livability outcomes for the city.

Pillar 4: Creating a smart Karachi. Great cities innovate with smart policies and smart solutions to manage city services; enhance competitiveness; facilitate stakeholder engagement and participation; use city assets creatively, efficiently, and sustainably; and make better project investments. Karachi can leverage information and communication technologies for planning and improving citizen services. E-governance platforms, if appropriately designed and implemented, can greatly enhance the efficiency, transparency, and convenience of services for businesses and citizens.

Recommendations for Reforms, Institutional Development, and Investments

The Karachi City Diagnostic has underlined the structural nature of the problems the city faces as it tries to improve its economy, livability, and inclusiveness. Failing to tackle these challenges in a timely and systematic manner would further exacerbate the urban infrastructure and service deficit in the city. A comprehensive programmatic, strategic, and phased approach is needed. Such an approach must be fully aligned with the Karachi Strategic Development Plan (KSDP) 2020 and would consist of four tracks.

Track 1: Create a shared vision. Envision a livable, inclusive, and sustainable metropolis with a joint commitment across federal, provincial, and city governments. Under this track, interventions can provide support surrounding the need to update the KSDP 2020 and a framework or platform to undertake participatory processes that involve all key stakeholders, including civil society, vulnerable groups such as women and youth, and the private sector.

Track 2: Improve institutional governance and performance. This entails strong coordination mechanisms among land-owning and service-delivery agencies, such as the Sindh Mass Transit Authority, Karachi Water and Sewerage Board, and Sindh Solid Waste Management Board. Under this track, interventions could support activities such as technical assistance as well as investments and goods acquisition aimed at increasing the city's ability to plan, fiscally position, and manage performance. Interventions can include reforms for accountability, strengthening of contractual agreements between province-level agencies and the city governments, and strengthening coordination among agencies.

Track 3: Enhance city management, planning, and the level of urban service delivery. Planning across different land-owning and service-delivery agencies, ensuring implementation and enforcement, and improving the management of and planning for public land for public benefit are essential. This track can include expenditures aimed at improving access to and quality of service delivery, in such areas as civil works in water and sanitation, urban and municipal road construction and maintenance, municipal solid waste, leveraging of the built heritage, public space development, safety and mobility, and green spaces management with a focus on disadvantaged neighborhoods. It can also include technical support for developing a citywide scope for engagement, such as through e-government platforms, enabling citizens to access key administrative services, provide feedback, and present grievances. Expenditures can also target municipal capacity to manage resources and assets, provide basic services, and enforce land-use and spatial planning and local development plans.

Track 4: Leverage financing, private participation, and competitiveness. Interventions can support municipal or provincial activities and reforms aimed at improving the ease of doing business and encouraging private sector partnerships. This can include identifying and addressing constraints to competitiveness and export in key sectors and prioritizing regulatory reforms. Activities can include technical assistance and investments aimed at speeding up processes and reducing discretionary power in key business transactions through the simplification and automation of procedures for creating and operating a business and related construction permits that fall under the city's or province's responsibility. This could be complemented with assistance to reform the sector's legal, regulatory, and financial policy frameworks that encourage private-sector involvement in urban infrastructure provision, with a focus on water and sanitation, urban transport, and solid waste. This track's interventions can also enhance cost recovery with careful social policies. These should consider that the current underpricing of municipal services is contributing to the financial weakness of utilities, slowing access expansion, and constraining the quality of service. This track can also include actions aimed at enhancing the collection of municipal utility taxes and service fees, reducing commercial and physical losses, and enhancing the value of existing city assets, which would entail proper operation and maintenance. Land assets and land use could be leveraged to facilitate growth, and at the same time better access to and transparency of property taxes and other municipal own-source revenue collection could be provided. Female labor force participation and related economic opportunities for women could also be increased in Karachi. This will require a greater understanding of specific factors constraining women in Karachi from joining the formal labor market and a recognition of the multidimensional barriers they face, including social norms, transport and mobility constraints, harassment in workplaces and public spaces, absence of gender-responsive infrastructure and facilities, and other barriers related to violence, security, and urbanization.

A summary of the detailed recommendations is provided in table 5.1.

Table 5.1 Summary of Detailed Recommendations

Area/sector	Recommendations	Relevant chapter in report
Urban planning and city development	Consolidate and disclose accurate city data as a first step toward effective integrated planning. This should be partnered with transparent development and real estate indicators, transactions, and processes and links to the property tax system.	3, under "Urban Planning and Policy"
	Regional planning should utilize benefits from China-Pakistan Economic Corridor for equitable, inclusive, and efficient economic and safeguard growth while safeguarding environmental and cultural assets.	
	Create formal coordination mechanism for various land-owning agencies at different levels of government operating in Karachi, to ensure coordinated and integrated city development.	
	Revise, update, and approve Karachi Strategic Development Plan 2020 to respond to current context, with concrete implementation modalities.	
	Explore transparent mechanisms for land disposal from public sector and allocate land to utilize this scare resource to meet demand.	
	Leverage city assets such as heritage buildings, waterfront, and public spaces to develop accessible and open spaces for improved civic and economic activity.	
	Incorporate plans to improve resilience to external shocks and possible impact of climate change in the city.	
City management and governance	Empower elected local governments to deliver services to the city.	3, under "City Management, Governance, and Institutional Capacity"
	Enhance mechanisms for accountability of local governments to citizens (to make them more inclusive) and the provincial government (for consistency and transparency of administration and oversight).	
	Implement sustained program to increase capacity of elected and appointed local officials in delivering their mandates.	
	Consider creating empowered master plan office as an independent body having representation from all land-owning agencies and technical experts.	
	Enhance formal coordination between KMC and DMCs following best practice models of metropolitan governance.	
	Create mechanism for inclusive city planning, with representation of women and other vulnerable groups so that any investment in the city responds to their needs.	

table continues next page

Table 5.1 Summary of Detailed Recommendations *(continued)*

Area/sector	Recommendations	Relevant chapter in report
Public transport and mass transit	**Short term** Ensure Sindh Mass Transit Authority has representation from city government. Improve management of existing urban road space by enhancing traffic management (recirculation, channelization, centralized traffic signaling); provide off-street parking and better enforcement. Improve nonmotorized transport environment by developing sidewalks, road crossings, bikeways, and so forth. Implement intelligent transport systems and use of cameras and sensors for traffic counts and emission monitoring. Generate open data and encourage innovation (apps development). Conduct traffic safety audit to identify major trouble spots that can be improved with small investment or minor traffic management. Conduct route rationalization of public transport routes to optimize existing transport fleet. **Medium to long term** Enable formal private sector financing for major investments in public transport systems, including bus rapid transit and rail systems, bus fleets, and so forth. Provide incentives to the existing transport operators to organize formally with easier access to financing for fleet modernization. Implement sustained program to increase capacity of public sector transport regulatory and development agencies. Invest in making public transport safe and reliable for women (and vulnerable groups), as they rely on public transport more than men but face substantial challenges.	3, under "Urban Transport"
Water and sewerage	**Short term** Transform KWSB into a modern utility to make it autonomous, professionally managed by qualified staff, with clear lines of accountability and customer focus. Develop a new KWSB strategy that outlines performance standards, capital investment needs, systems, procedures and equipment deficits, training needs, institutional optimization, and staff and management incentive structures. Improve operating environment within KWSB by restructuring KWSB board; establishing a pro-poor unit and developing a pro-poor strategy; and appointing an NRW team and associated NRW reduction strategy. Revisit financial sustainability arrangements with provincial and municipal partners. Improve consultation and outreach with stakeholders toward meaningful citizen engagement, by developing a communications strategy, doing regular consultation and feedback to develop a turnaround package with broad support, establishing grievances redress mechanisms, and investing in improved customer relations. Establish "net demand" for water. (Net demand for water is the volume for water needed if NRW levels are reduced to international best practice standards for a comparable metropolis.) This includes several specific actions that KWSB needs to carry out—listed in chapter 3.	3, under "Water Supply and Sanitation"

table continues next page

Transforming Karachi into a Livable and Competitive Megacity
http://dx.doi.org/10.1596/978-1-4648-1211-8

Table 5.1 Summary of Detailed Recommendations *(continued)*

Area/sector	Recommendations	Relevant chapter in report
	Formulate long-term sector policy and set up accountability arrangements, including outlining how GoS will support KWSB and how KWSB will evolve to deliver services.	
	Medium to long term	
	Invest in pumping efficiency improvement and rehabilitation.	
	Improve pro-poor service levels to focus on improving service for residents of low-income communities.	
	Invest in network rehabilitation and sewerage expansion. Priority investments may include replacement and/or rehabilitation of trunk mains, distribution network and large pumping stations, and sewerage projects, network improvements, and rehabilitation and construction of treatment plants.	
	Finance a long-term investment program that prioritizes water transfer and distribution. This may include subsequent phases of K-IV water transfer investments and expansion and rehabilitation of large filtration plans.	
Solid waste management	**Short term**	3, under "Municipal Solid Waste"
	Review legal framework for solid waste management and clarify responsibilities between local governments and Sindh Solid Waste Management Board. Create contracts of agreement between the two that specify roles, responsibilities, funding, and authorities.	
	Develop investment program focusing on transfer stations and sanitary landfills, including closure of official dump sites.	
	Introduce reforms to upgrade cost recovery and developing markets for waste by-products, including the following: fees, pricing policies for renewable energy and compost, and preferential procurement incentives for recyclables and recovered resources.	
	Introduce reforms to transition systems to licensed private service providers instead of government-paid contractors, especially for types of waste considered viable in the private market or with potential for private participation, including the following: hazardous or infectious medical waste, cattle feedlot manure, construction and demolition debris, and industrial waste from large generators.	
	Conduct the following site investigation activities for transfer station and landfill sites: geotechnical and topographic conditions of transfer station sites; preliminary environmental impact assessments (EIAs) for transfer station sites; design-build-operate-transfer tender documents; social inclusion studies of informal workers in waste recycling, including people living at dumpsites; and feasibility studies and preliminary EIAs for sanitary landfills.	

table continues next page

Table 5.1 Summary of Detailed Recommendations *(continued)*

Area/sector	Recommendations	Relevant chapter in report
	Medium term	
	Develop procurement strategy and detailed technical studies of the following: design-build-operate (DBO) concession contracts for transfer stations; detailed designs for sanitary landfills, including mitigation measures to address EIA findings and closure activities for waste dumped onto small portions of selected sites; tender documents for DBO concession contracts for sanitary landfills; feasibility study of rail transport of waste to the eastern sanitary landfill; tender documents for DBO concession contracts of rail transport, if viable; market studies and pricing requirements for recycling and resource recovery facilities at sanitary landfills, initially as pilots to confirm viability; DBO concession contract tender documents for recycling and resource recovery facilities, initially as pilots to confirm viability; feasibility studies and DBO concession (possibly public-private partnership versus outsourced private service provider contract) for hospital and cattle farm waste.	
Public financing for investment and service delivery	**Urban property tax**	4, under "Fiscal Risks to Sustainability"
	Update and modernize entire Urban Immovable Property Tax system by conducting the following activities: comprehensive survey of properties in entire cities; digitization, computerization, and automation of property tax system; increase in tax net coverage by notifying all built-up urban areas as rating areas; updating of valuation tables to reflect market values of land; reducing differential between owner-occupied and rental property; levying full property tax on developed vacant land to discourage speculative plot holdings; and releasing land for productive uses.	
	Local government financing	
	Improve fiscal resources available to local governments by revising and updating the fiscal transfer mechanism (Provincial Financial Commission Award) for local governments based on international best practices, to ensure that allocations are based on needs, functions, and size, along with other development criteria; creating mechanism for performance-based grants; and ensuring predictable, scheduled, and automatic fiscal transfers from province to local governments.	
	Improve financial management in local governments by improving budgetary practices (budget forecasting and synchronizing to a medium-term framework); increasing own-source revenue collections for local governments by helping them increase tax base, rationalize rates and fees, update methods of billing and collection, conduct communication campaigns, and so forth; and improving transparency, disclosure, and auditing practices by developing detailed financial statements and requiring local governments to take steps to address pending audit observations.	
Environment, disaster risks, and climate resilience	**Short term**	4, under "Environmental Sustainability and Climate Change Risks"
	Conduct vulnerability assessment of critical and essential facilities, such as road links, bridges, health facilities, schools, and public offices.	

table continues next page

Table 5.1 Summary of Detailed Recommendations *(continued)*

Area/sector	Recommendations	*Relevant chapter in report*
	Reinforce emergency management response capacity by undertaking the following: developing integrated citywide emergency management plans; renovating and outfitting city-level disaster risk management facilities; building and outfitting city-level District Disaster Management Authorities, fire service, and emergency response facilities; supplying, installing, and integrating specialized emergency management and communications technology equipment within local-level agencies; supplying specialized search-and-rescue equipment to local-level agencies for scaling up existing interventions such as Rescue 1299; and providing training, exercises, and drills to local-level agencies.	
	Improve land-use planning and building control to incorporate disaster risk resilience by integrating risk information into city development planning; improve processes and capacity at Sindh Building Control Authority, KMC, Karachi Development Authority, and other relevant agencies to incorporate disaster risk in developing, approving, and enforcing land-use plans and building control regulations at the level of zoning, site, and building plans.	
	Medium to long term	
	"Green" public infrastructure to ensure that all new investments in infrastructure and services have minimal environmental footprint and encourage reduction of emissions.	
	Develop environmental infrastructure such as common effluent treatment plants for liquid industrial waste, wastewater treatment plants for domestic effluents, and associated laboratory facilities for quality control.	
Social inclusion	**Short term**	4, under "Social Risks to Sustainability"
	Citizen engagement: develop citizen feedback mechanisms such as citizen scorecards, e-government platform, and grievance redress mechanisms for services.	
	Urban youth-targeted social programs: these should aim to reduce violence by providing safe spaces and healthy alternative activities for youth in urban areas, by supporting music groups, sports teams, and other social and cultural activities.	
	Employment-intensive infrastructure programs: invest in infrastructure projects focusing on unplanned and least-privileged areas with an emphasis on providing employment for local communities, specifically for young men.	
	Medium to long term	
	Invest in public spaces to promote social interaction, community building, and economic exchange. Special focus should be given to needs of women and other usually excluded and vulnerable groups living in or using these spaces.	

table continues next page

Table 5.1 Summary of Detailed Recommendations *(continued)*

Area/sector	Recommendations	Relevant chapter in report
	Enhance female labor force participation by designing interventions aimed at relieving women's constraints on entering the labor force. Such interventions include adequate, reliable, and safe public transport for women; gender-responsive facilities in the public and private sectors (affordable day care centers, working women's hostels, and so forth) and safer public spaces.	
	Improve safety and security for women in Karachi through measures such as establishment of more women-only police stations or allocation of women-specific desks in all police stations.	

Note: DMC = District Municipal Corporation; KMC = Karachi Metropolitan Corporation; KWSB = Karachi Water and Sewerage Board; NRW = nonrevenue water.

Enabling Private-Sector Financing to Meet Karachi's Infrastructure Needs

Chapter 4 highlighted that inadequate availability of financing is a key constraint on reducing the large and growing infrastructure and service-delivery gaps in Karachi. Karachi needs an estimated US$9 billion–US$10 billion in financing over a 10-year period to meet these gaps in three sectors: urban transport, water supply, and sanitation and municipal solid waste. Current infrastructure spending by the public sector in Karachi is well below these requirements, despite large recent increases. The solution is to leverage significant and diverse sources of financing—both public and private.

Provincial and local governments have three general types of instruments to meet Karachi's financing needs: (i) fiscal transfers from higher levels of government, (ii) their own sources of revenue, and (iii) instruments for leveraging other sources of financing (see figure 5.1).

Figure 5.1 Various Financial Instruments to Finance Capital Investments in Karachi

	① Fiscal transfer instruments	② Own-source revenue instruments	③ Leveraging instruments	
Current: efficiency & expansion	Block grants Targeted conditional transfers	Urban property taxes Tariffs and fees	**Borrowing** Direct bank borrowing *(small-scale loans)*	**Investments** Management contracts
Future potential	Performance grants Guarantees	Land-value capture instruments	Municipal bond market *(local or international)* Credit enhancements-MIGA IFC municipal finance products	PPPs Special-purpose vehicles Infrastructure funds

In the short and medium terms, the government can expand and improve efficiency by using the (i) urban property tax, (ii) conditional fiscal transfers to municipal governments, and (iii) management contracts with the private sector for service delivery.

In the long term, the government must leverage other sources of financing via reforms and innovations. These include (i) explicit performance-based grants for municipal governments; (ii) instruments for land-value capture—to share in the benefits of increases in private land and property values as a result of infrastructure improvements, especially around planned mass transit stations; (iii) subnational or municipal bonds or enhanced credit or loan options with access guarantees (such as those issued by sovereign entities or multilateral organizations) to obtain private or institutional financing; and (iv) innovative public-private partnerships, special-purpose vehicles, and infrastructure funds to invest in Karachi's needs.

The following are some of the constraints hindering commercial, private, and institutional investment in infrastructure and service delivery in Karachi. The government will need to alleviate these constraints to leverage and mobilize private financing to meet the city's needs:

- Perceived high risk due to a weak policy framework and regulations
- High risk of insecurity and weakening law and order
- Low capacity of public institutions to regulate and encourage private investment
- High cost of doing business for the private sector
- The prevalence of a large informal sector in every economic and service sector
- Low precedent of formal private financing for infrastructure
- A weak or absent subnational borrowing framework
- Absence of adequate risk-sharing mechanisms for various types of risks facing infrastructure investments

World Bank Enterprise Survey
Key Findings

Figure A.1 Firms' Ratings of Biggest Obstacles to Business, Sindh Province versus Other Countries, 2013

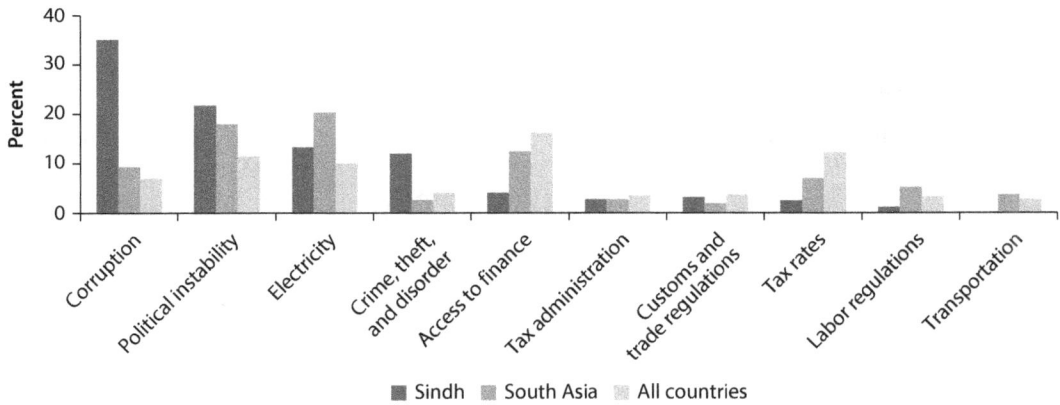

Figure A.2 Firms' Ratings of Biggest Obstacles to Business, Comparison of Provinces, 2013

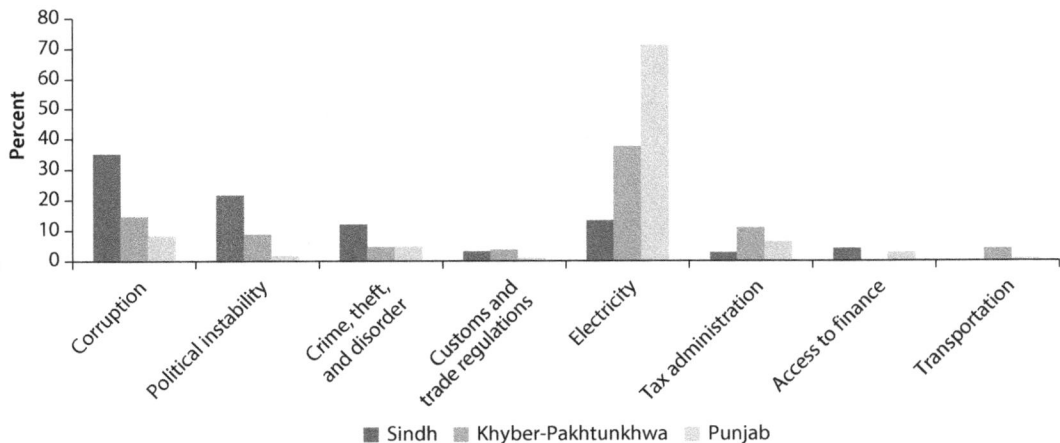

Figure A.3 Firms' Ratings of Biggest Obstacles to Business, Sindh, 2007 versus 2013

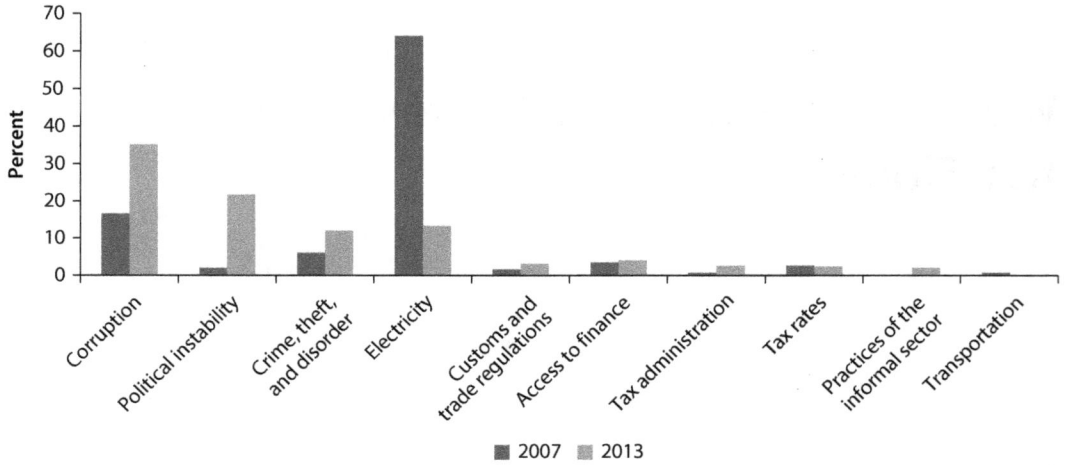

Sources: For all tables, DfID n.d.; World Bank and IFC 2015.

References

DfID (Department for International Development). N.d. "Investment Climate Core Brief." DfID internal document. London.

World Bank and IFC (International Finance Corporation). 2015. "Enterprise Surveys: Pakistan Country Profile 2013." Washington, DC: World Bank and IFC.

World Bank *Doing Business* Key Findings

Figure B.1 Trade across Borders: Compliance Time

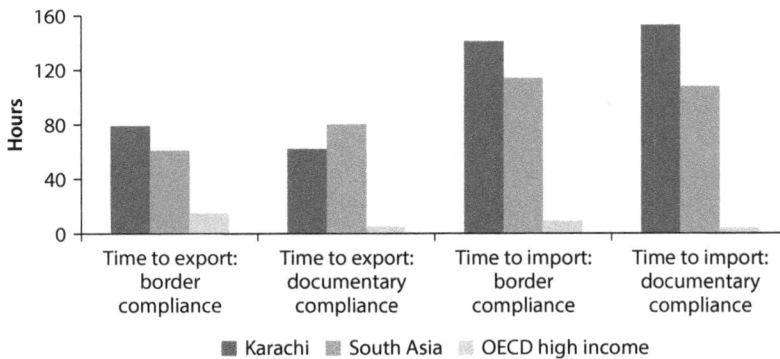

Note: OECD = Organisation for Economic Co-operation and Development.

Figure B.2 Paying Taxes: Number of Payments and Time Involved

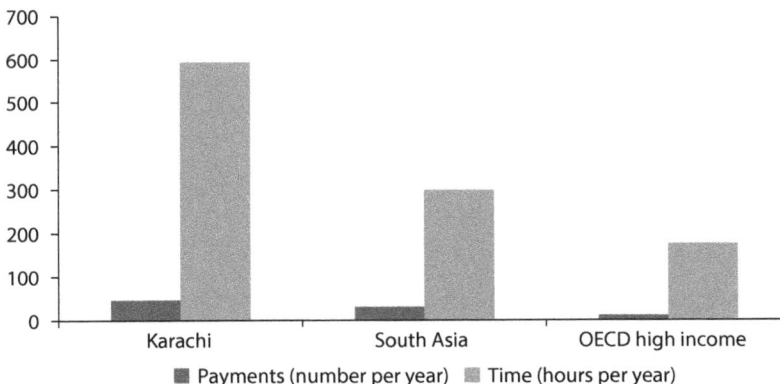

Note: OECD = Organisation for Economic Co-operation and Development.

Table B.1 Karachi: Subnational Doing Business Rankings

Topic rankings	Rank among 13 cities in Pakistan	Top city in Pakistan
Starting a business	3	Islamabad
Dealing with construction permits	10	Multan
Registering property	11	Faisalabad, Sialkot
Paying taxes	11	Islamabad
Trading across borders	1	Karachi
Enforcing contracts	3	Sukkur

Sources: All tables and figures, World Bank 2010, 2012.

References

World Bank. 2010. *Doing Business in Pakistan 2010*. Washington, DC: World Bank.

———. 2012. *Doing Business 2012: Doing Business in a More Transparent World*. Washington, DC. World Bank.

Land-Use Cover Maps of Karachi, 2001 and 2013

Map C.1 Karachi Land Use, 2001

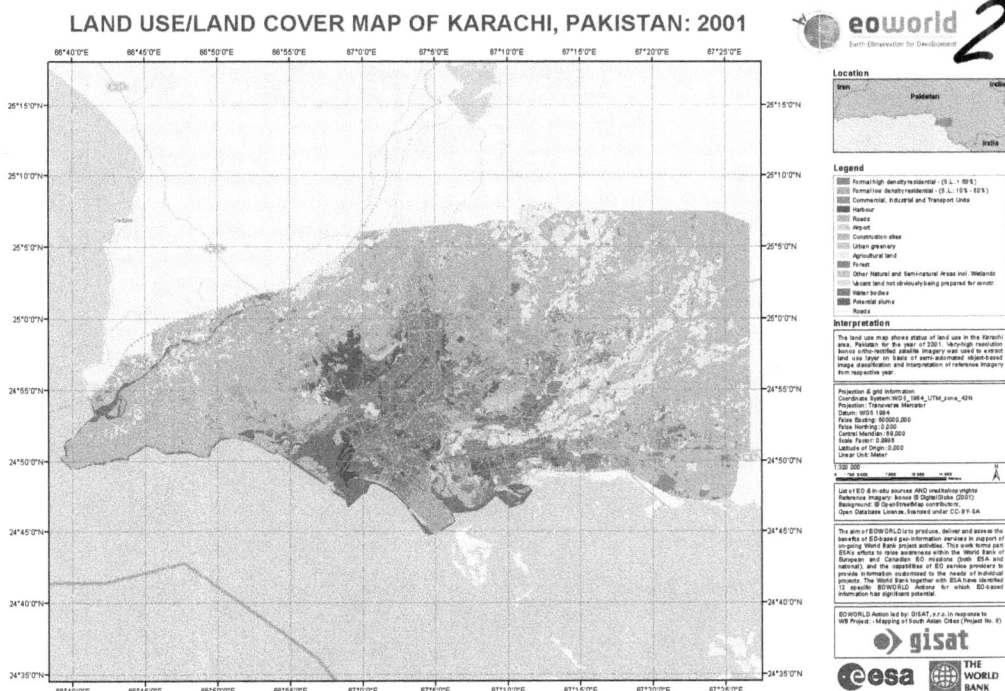

Map C.2 Karachi Land Use, 2013

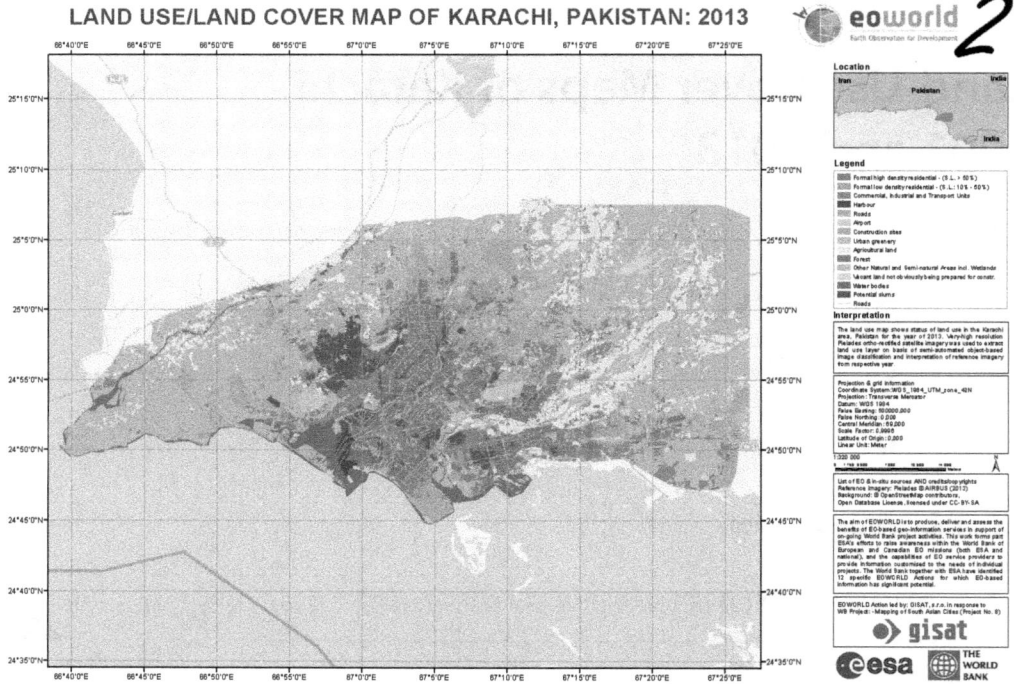

LAND USE/LAND COVER MAP OF KARACHI, PAKISTAN: 2013

Planning and City Management Case Studies

Singapore's Planning, Land Management, and Implementation Framework

Land is a scarce resource in Singapore. With slightly more than 719 square kilometers supporting a growing population of about 5.5 million, the city-state has invested heavily in planning to balance competing land uses and meet the needs and aspirations of its people. It has put in place an integrated planning and development framework that guides plans at the national and local levels. The framework addresses public-private partnerships, the supply of land, and development control, among other factors. The statutory master plan typically includes detailed land-use standards to safeguard and accommodate existing infrastructure and growth areas in areas such as commerce, industry, housing, amenities, open space and greenery, transportation networks, and infrastructure. (See figure D.1.) Beyond specifying land use and density for developments, the master plan contains detailed layers to further shape the spatial structure of the city: plans for parks and bodies of water; landed properties; building heights; activity-generating uses; and street blocks, urban design, conservation areas, and monuments (Singapore Urban Redevelopment Authority 2014a).

Inclusive Urban Planning and City Revitalization in Medellín

Medellín, the second-largest city in Colombia, has experienced rapid growth since the middle of the 20th century, from a population of about 358,000 in 1951 to an estimated 2.44 million in 2013.

Its metropolitan region consists of more than 3.5 million people spread across the Aburrá Valley. In the 1990s, Medellín's reputation was as the world's murder capital. This characterization turned around when, in 2004, the city underwent radical urban revitalization under the leadership of Mayor Sergio Fajardo. Medellín enhanced law enforcement and initiated a series of innovative public investments. Fajardo led a process of community involvement in the planning

Figure D.1 Singapore's Planning, Land Management, and Implementation Framework

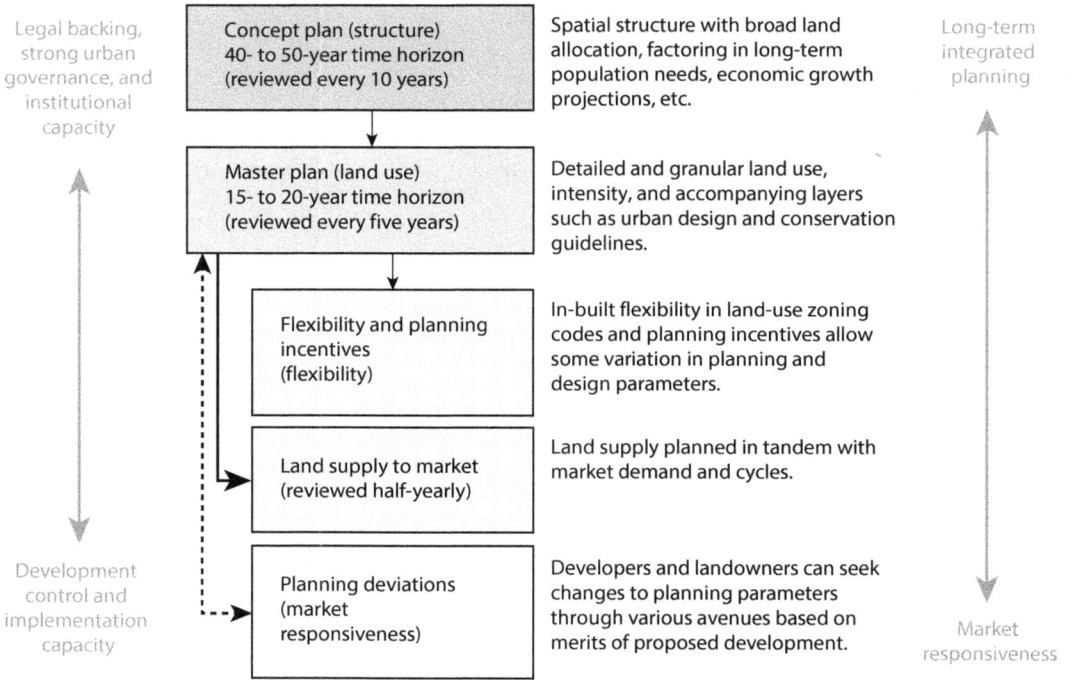

Source: Singapore Urban Redevelopment Authority 2014b.

and design of these investments, as well as public participation in municipal funds allocation. The investments in public works focused on the poorest and most violent areas. Many of these projects were designed to integrate the city's low-income residents and communities with its commercial center.

In 2014, the municipal government spent 85 percent of its US$2.2 billion budget on infrastructure and services for the poorest parts of the city. That spending included community programs, public transportation, and modern architecture. A metrorail system opened in 1995, linking the north and south of the Aburrá Valley. To connect the poorest districts, the city later built two aerial cable-car lines. It used the system stations as anchors for "integrated urban plans"—a combination of new buildings (such as libraries, schools, and galleries); public spaces (such as concert venues and parks); and social programs. It has since built 120 schools and nine signature library parks. A third of the city's budget is allocated to education.

The revitalization and social urbanism project was paid for by revenues from the city's ownership of its utility company. Since its creation in the 1950s, Empresas Publicas de Medellín has transferred approximately 30 percent of its annual profits to the municipality for social investment projects. And while gang violence and homicides have not disappeared, they are remarkably lower than in the 1990s. Inequality and unemployment remain key challenges for the city, but because of the vision of its leadership and the buy-in of its citizens, Medellín was named the Urban Land Institute's Most Innovative City in 2013.

References

Singapore Urban Redevelopment Authority. 2014a. "Ensuring a Stable and Sustainable Property Market." https://www.ura.gov.sg/uol.

———. 2014b. "Our Planning Process." https://www.ura.gov.sg/uol/concept-plan/our -planning-process/our-planning-process.aspx.

Transforming Karachi into a Livable and Competitive Megacity
http://dx.doi.org/10.1596/978-1-4648-1211-8

APPENDIX E

Fragmentation of Land Control in Karachi

Table E.1 Characteristics of Land Ownership and Control in Karachi Division

Level	Characteristics	Agency	Land area (% of Karachi Division)
Federal (12.3%)	Large prime tracks of land in city core. Own building bylaws and development programs	Defense Housing Authority (DHA)	5.0
		Karachi Port Trust (KPT)	2.8
		Cantonment Board	2.1
		Port Qasim	1.5
		Government of Pakistan	0.5
		Railways	0.4
Province (48.5%)	Large tracks inland and on periphery. National park outside city	Kirthar National Park	21.7
		Government of Sindh	17.7
		Layari Development Authority (LDA)	5.6
		Malir Development Authority (MLA)	3.9
		Sindh Industrial Trading Estate (SITE)	0.6
Local (32.7%)	Fragmented and dispersed throughout city	Karachi Metropolitan Corporation (KMC)/city government	30.9
		Cooperative Housing Societies	1.8
Others (6.6%)		Private	3.9
		Recent allocations (e.g., industrial, educational)	2.7

Source: City District Government Karachi, "Karachi Strategic Development Plan 2020," 2007.

Water Supply and Sanitation Case Studies

Institutional and Governance Reform in Peshawar, Khyber Pakhtunkhwa

In September 2014, the government of Khyber Pakhtunkhwa (GoKP) in Pakistan took a bold step and established Pakistan's first corporate-governed and autonomous utility in Peshawar. Water and Sanitation Services Peshawar is a 100 percent GoKP-owned public utility, with a diverse board of directors and professional managers delivering municipal services to the 2.3 million citizens of Peshawar. The World Bank supported GoKP from 2011 to 2014 in designing and implementing governance and institutional reform, which is delivering results. The transformation process transformed seven fragmented water and sanitation municipal utilities into one citywide autonomous, professionally managed, and ring-fenced utility incorporated with the Securities and Exchange Commission of Pakistan under the 1984 Companies Ordinance.

Use of Performance-Based Leakage Reduction in Ho Chi Minh City, Vietnam

Ho Chi Minh City (HCMC) is the commercial capital of Vietnam, with a population of more than 9 million. In HCMC, the Saigon Water Company (SAWACO) delivers drinking water. In 2004, diagnostic work established that there was 41 percent nonrevenue water in SAWACO, of which 90 percent came from leakages through service connections. The World Bank supported SAWACO in designing and implementing a performance-based leakage reduction contract to lower leakage in one zone in the city using a public-private partnership model. The contract comprises the design and construction of a district metering area, on a traditional unit-cost basis, followed by leakage reduction paid on a fixed fee and performance basis. The fixed fee was set at a maximum of around 30 percent (70 percent of contractor remuneration is contingent on demonstrated water savings), with the performance payment made for every cubic meter of water saved.

Independent verification was used to confirm the leakage reductions. The results have been impressive. The contract was awarded to Manila Water Company in mid-2008. Within three years, almost 40,000 cubic meters per day (m^3/day) of water were being saved, against a target of 20,000 m^3/day. At the end of the five-year contract, the contractor was saving 121,000 m^3/day against a target of 37,500 m^3/day. This is sufficient water to provide service to an additional 300,000 people. Further, hydraulic pressures in the network have increased, and additional income of over US$4 million has resulted.

Manila Water Company, the Philippines

Manila Water Company operates a 25-year concession for water and wastewater services in Metro Manila's East Zone, a 1,400-square-kilometer area that is home to over 6 million people.

The government of the Philippines decided to privatize Manila's water system in 1997 to address uneven access to piped water and sanitation systems in the capital. International Finance Corporation (IFC) advisory services acted as lead adviser for the privatization, designing the operating agreement and overseeing the bidding process for the concessionaire.

Six years later, in 2003, after a due diligence process to ensure that there was no conflict of interest following the advisory engagement, IFC investment services provided a $30 million loan to Manila Water Company, which was followed in 2004 by a $30 million loan and a $15 million equity investment. The company was listed on the Philippine Stock Exchange in 2005.

Over the past two decades, Manila Water Company has significantly improved the quality of water and sanitation services in the East Manila area, with $1.5 billion in investments, including the laying of more than 4,000 kilometers of water pipes. These investments extended the reach of water coverage to 99 percent of the population, up from 26 percent before services were privatized. Many of the people not previously connected to water services were members of poor families who were paying local water sellers $3 per cubic meter of water. Today, the average tariff in Manila is $1.30, and the poorest residents pay a lower, subsidized rate.

Assessment of the Current System of Solid Waste Management in Karachi

No Systematic Management of Street Sweeping

Most street sweeping in Karachi is performed manually, with a few mechanical sweepers on some main roads. There is no standardization of road length to be swept by a sweeper and no logical plans or intervals for sweeping streets. At some locations, sweepers are assigned according to road length or population density. As a result, an extensive amount of waste remains on roads, open spaces, and canals, affecting drainage. This has a deleterious impact on health and disease transmission.

Gaps in Refuse Collection

In addition to door-to-door collection in wealthier areas, there are 4,085 distributed communal bins that are emptied on a scheduled or as-needed basis. A total of 4,170 employees are involved in service delivery. There is still a significant gap in collection, with 8,000 tons per day disposed of illegally and informally.

Inefficiencies in Waste Collection

Despite having 567 vehicles for waste collection, 25 percent are inoperable at any given time. Vehicles travel 60 kilometers round-trip on their route to two approved dump sites in heavy traffic, increasing collection costs.[1] In addition, some collection vehicles take their waste to specified locations for consolidation and on-transport by larger vehicles to dump sites. However, this waste is often scavenged for recyclables and burned. The idea of transfer stations is a good one, but needs further exploration.[2]

Existing Disposal Sites Estimated to Be Filled by 2016

Jam Charko (500 acres), located in the north part of Gadap town, is 25 kilometers away from Karachi's business district. The site has been operating since 1990 and is estimated to be full in 2016. Gond Pass (500 acres) is located to the northwest of the town of Baldia, three kilometers from the Hub River and 27 kilometers from Karachi's business district. Gond Pass site's life is unknown, but some have estimated that 2016 saw the site full. There are reported issues at the sites—for example, that contractors are not paid on time.

Recycling Rate Low and Not Captured

About 11,000 people take part in the recycling of paper, glass, cardboard, and plastic, much of which is exported through intermediaries for profit. Recycling takes place in five stages within the existing system: (i) in the household, (ii) by the rubbish collector, (iii) at the community bin, (iv) at informal transfer stations, and (v) at the landfill site (there are about 1,000 pickers at each of the two sites). It is estimated that less than 5 percent of the waste generated is recycled. The revenue received from recycling is not known, but none is captured to be reinvested in the system.

Notes

1. More data are needed to analyze the economic efficiency of this model.
2. This was noted in the Karachi Strategic Development Plan 2020, published in 2007, which recommended that six transfer stations be built at locations that have been designated for this purpose. However, further work is needed to confirm the environmental validity and social impact of these plans.

Potential Private-Sector Involvement in Karachi

LED Street Lighting

Public-private partnerships (PPPs) to provide street lighting are becoming increasingly common, given the level of efficiency that can be achieved with private-sector participation. A street-lighting PPP project in Karachi would entail replacing existing energy-inefficient lamps along the major roads of the city with light-emitting diode (LED) street lights, which is likely to achieve energy savings of 50–80 percent. If implemented, this can be a simple improvement in public services that generates long-term cost savings. The project can initially be implemented in select areas of the city and replicated in other parts.

Rooftop Solar Projects

Karachi is an ideal market for harvesting solar energy, given its abundant supply of sunshine—as much as 3,100 hours annually. Additionally, with the declining prices of solar panels, solar projects have now become more attractive as methods to curtail energy expenditure, especially for the municipal government. Hence, opportunities exist for private-sector participation in small solar rooftop projects similar to successful projects in India. For example, in 2012, the International Finance Corporation helped the local government of the capital of the state of Gujarat—Gandhinagar—to attract private-sector participation for the installation of photovoltaic panels on the roofs of selected public buildings as well as private residences and for connecting them to the grid.

Waste Management

Karachi produces approximately 20,000 tons of solid waste every day, out of which only 2,000 tons are transported to the landfill sites situated outside Karachi. The remaining waste is burned within the city and/or dumped in the two main drainage channels—the Lyari and Malir rivers—that are now spewing garbage, along with other, smaller drains and open dumps situated in and around residential areas. Opportunities, therefore, exist to attract private-sector participation to the waste management space—particularly within waste collection, transportation, treatment, and disposal—as well as to the production of energy from solid waste. K-Electric is currently implementing a solid waste–to–energy project that is expected to reduce the waste that remains dumped in the open or in small landfills and dumping areas that exist everywhere in Karachi.

Urban Transport

The urban public transport problem in Karachi is worsening every day, with rapid increases in population and a lack of investment in urban transport by successive governments. According to a 2009 study conducted by the Japan International Cooperation Agency, vehicle ownership in 2020 was estimated at 61.6 percent due to poor urban transport infrastructure. Assuming that an average household has 3.9 members, the same study estimated that there will be 7 million households in Karachi by the year 2020, and the number of vehicles owned will be nearly 4.3 million. This comes to 156 vehicles for every 1,000 people.

Although some efforts are under way by the provincial government to improve the capacity of public transport in Karachi, such as the Bus Rapid Transit System (BRTS) Blue Line Project, the government does not have the fiscal capacity to solve the issue of lack of public transport on its own. It is, therefore, imperative for the government to introduce private-sector participation within the construction, operations, and maintenance of urban transport systems, such as BRTS (Yellow and Orange lines), Karachi Circular Railway, and so forth.

Automated Record Management System

Most government records, such as land registry and vehicle registration, are still kept on paper, which is vulnerable to fire, theft, and so forth. Automating records management will not only reduce the burden of records responsibilities on individuals but also make the process more efficient and transparent and improve the accountability of information. Given the fiscal constraint on the government in undertaking this automation process, these services could be outsourced to the private sector under the terms of a concession.

Potable Water

Almost all of Karachi's water supply comes from two main sources: Keenjhar Lake, about 120 kilometers to the northeast of the city; and Hub Dam, which is 60 kilometers toward the northwest. The original design capacity of both sources stood at 583 million gallons per day (MGD) and 100 MGD, respectively, but these have decreased considerably due to poor upkeep of water-transporting machinery and, in the case of Hub Dam, a paucity of rainfall. Moreover, Karachi requires 1,000 MGD, and 25 percent of the water supplied to Karachi is pilfered at various sources. One of the ways to address this issue is to introduce a private-sector role in water management and supply, similar to what has been done in Manila.

Transforming Karachi into a Livable and Competitive Megacity
http://dx.doi.org/10.1596/978-1-4648-1211-8

Karachi Strategic Development Plan 2020

Karachi's spatial growth strategy and proposed land-use plan show large housing schemes on the periphery and commercial and mixed-use areas within the inner city, as shown in map I.1.

Map I.1 Growth and Land Use in Karachi

a. Spatial growth strategy

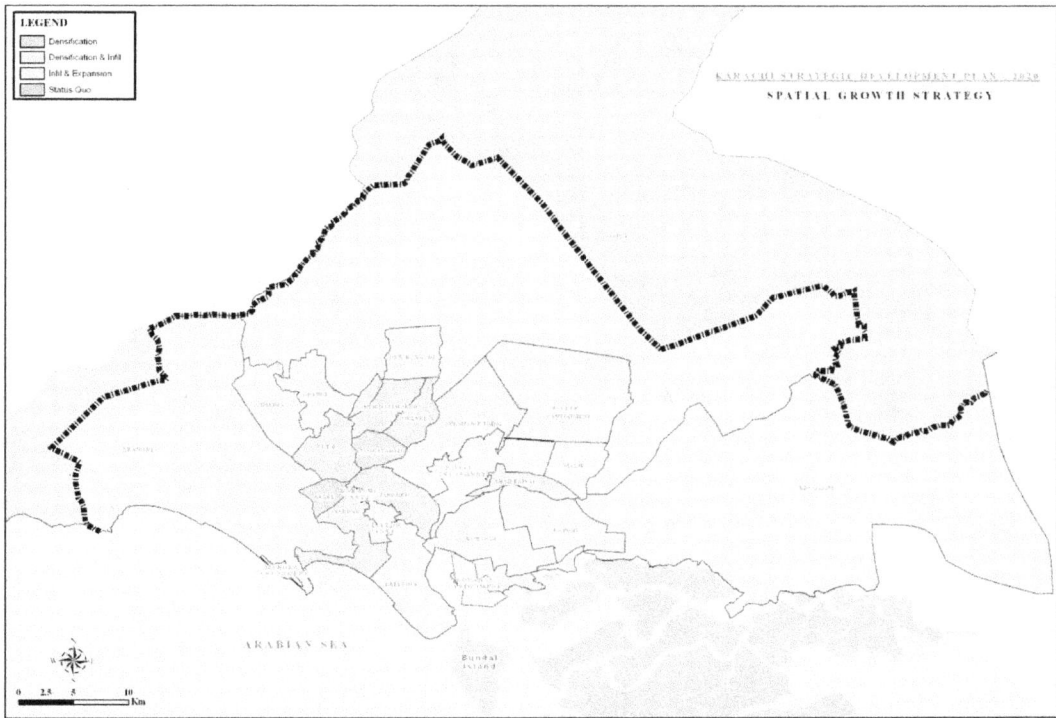

map continues next page

Map I.1 Growth and Land Use in Karachi *(continued)*

b. Proposed land-use plan

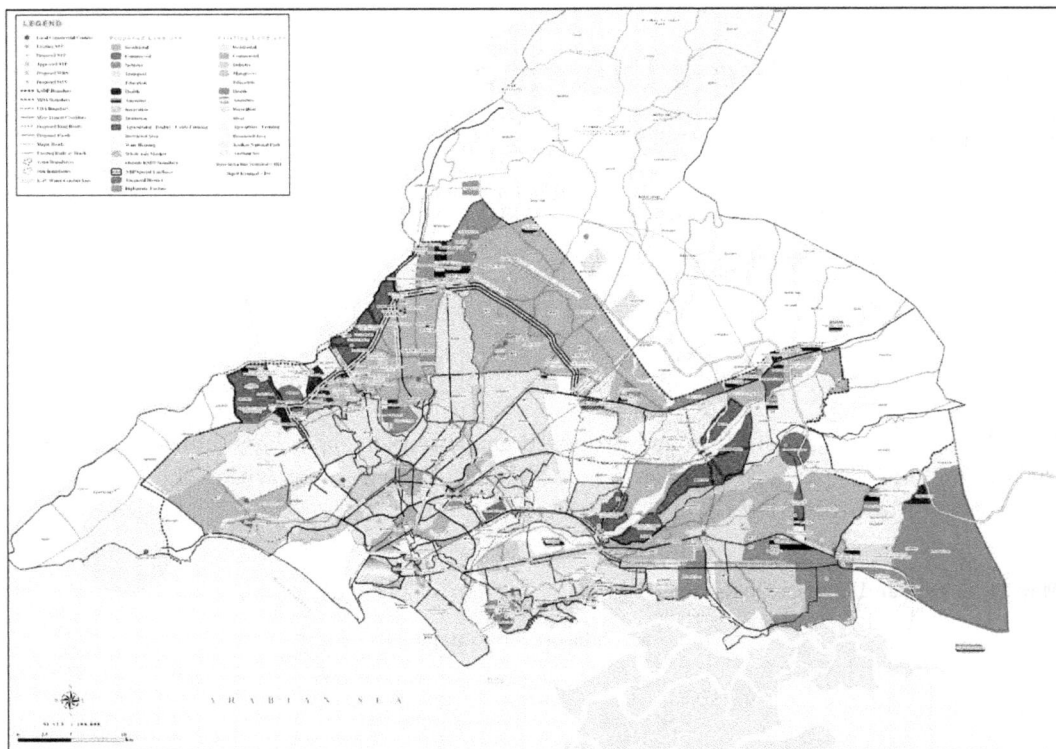

Source: Karachi Strategic Development Plan 2020.

Snapshot of the Prevailing Local Government System in Karachi

This appendix provides a snapshot of functions and responsibilities of city governments in Karachi under the Sindh Local Government Act (SLGA) 2013 and the prevailing local government system.

City governments in Karachi are structured on the model of metropolitan governance, with a metropolitan entity for the entire city area and district-level municipal entities under it. These are (i) the Karachi Metropolitan Corporation (KMC), headed by an elected mayor and deputy mayor at the metropolitan level; and (ii) six District Municipal Corporations (DMCs), headed by elected chairmen and vice chairmen at the district level. These collectively provide municipal functions in the urban areas of Karachi Division.

The SLGA divides municipal functions between the KMC and DMCs, with a selected number of higher-level and interdistrict functions being performed by the KMC (such as major roads and city-level infrastructure, large public amenities, parks and public spaces, major health care facilities, and so forth) and numerous municipal functions being the mandate of DMCs (such as solid waste management, street lighting, and community services). The SLGA stipulates that in case of overlap of functions between the KMC and DMCs, the KMC's mandate will take precedence and it will provide that function. However, unlike the standard metropolitan governance model, there is no formal coordination or relationship between the KMC and DMCs, creating another hindrance in city governance.

The KMC is responsible for the following:

1. Development planning
2. Development of interdistrict roads, bridges, street lights, and storm-water drains
3. Special development programs
4. Coordination, monitoring, and supervision of all interdistrict development work
5. Management of abattoirs and cattle colonies
6. Running of various specialized medical institutions and colleges

7. Maintaining large entertainment, recreation, and cultural areas for public use
8. Coordination of municipal wards and watches
9. Coordination of firefighting service
10. Management of civil defense and emergency response
11. Traffic engineering; coordinating milk supply schemes
12. Controlling land owned by the KMC and removal of encroachments from KMC properties
13. Any other function the government of Sindh (GoS) may assign.

The DMCs are responsible for the following:

1. Public health, which includes sanitation, removal, collection, and disposal of refuse (solid waste management and public toilets)
2. Water supply and drainage (in areas not in control of the Karachi Water and Sewerage Board) and regulating private sources of water supply
3. Public streets and street lighting
4. Traffic planning
5. Development planning (community development projects)
6. Primary and adult education
7. Regulation of food and drink
8. Management of slaughterhouses
9. Establishment of public markets and regulation of private markets for food and drink or sale of animals
10. Trees, parks, public gardens, open spaces, and nurseries
11. Cultural events, libraries, and entertainment events
12. Social welfare—welfare homes and institutions for the marginalized
13. Regulation of dangerous trades
14. Registration of birth, deaths, and marriages
15. Prevention of infectious diseases
16. Regulation of burial places, such as graveyards
17. Land development and improvement schemes of land owned by DMCs
18. Public housing schemes
19. Medical aid and relief
20. Any other function that GoS may assign

However, GoS retains substantial control over these local governments, which limits their autonomy. GoS authority over cities includes (i) appointment and replacement of all major officials in the city (including municipal commissioners); (ii) final approval of annual budgets; (iii) final approval of bylaws; (iv) final approval of tax proposals; (v) inspections, inquiries, and audits; and (vi) approval to let the city borrow or give a guarantee, among others. In addition, GoS has in the recent past taken over several key municipal and urban functions and removed them from the mandate of the city. These include master planning, building controls, solid waste management, and the development of peri-urban and peripheral lands. The city's water and sewerage utility is already under the administrative control of GoS.